D1326551

Compendium

of the

CATECHISM
OF THE
CATHOLIC
CHURCH

CATHOLIC TRUTH SOCIETY
PUBLISHERS TO THE HOLY SEE

The design of the logo on the cover is taken from a Christian tombstone in the catacombs of Domitilla in Rome, which dates from the end of the third century A.D.

This pastoral image, of pagan origin, was used by Christians to symbolise the rest and the happiness that the soul of the departed finds in eternal life.

This image also suggests certain characteristic aspects of this Compendium: Christ, the Good Shepherd, who leads and protects his faithful (the lamb) by his authority (the staff), draws them by the melodious symphony of the truth (the panpipes) and makes them lie down in the shade of the 'tree of life', his redeeming Cross which opens paradise.

The Compendium of the Cathechism of the Catholic Church: Published 2006 by the Incorporated Catholic Truth Society, 40–46 Harleyford Road, London, SE11 5AY Tel: 020 7640 0042 Fax: 020 7640 0046. Copyright © 2006 The Incorporated Catholic Truth Society in the format and design of this edition.

website: www.cts-online.org.uk

ISBN 1 86082 376 9

CONTENTS

PART TWO

THE CELEBRATION
OF THE CHRISTIAN MYSTERY

PART THREE
LIFE IN CHRIST

MOTU PROPRIO

for the approval and publication
of the *Compendium*
of the *Catechism of the Catholic Church*

To my Venerable Brothers the Cardinals, Patriarchs, Archbishops, Bishops, Priests, Deacons and to all the People of God.

Twenty years ago, work began on the *Catechism of the Catholic Church* that had been requested by the extraordinary Assembly of the Synod of Bishops held on the occasion of the twentieth anniversary of the close of the Second Vatican Council.

I am filled with heartfelt thanks to the Lord God for having given the Church this *Catechism*, promulgated in 1992 by my venerated and beloved Predecessor, Pope John Paul II.

The great value and beauty of this gift are confirmed above all by the extensive and positive reception of the *Catechism* among bishops, to whom it was primarily addressed as a sure and authentic reference text for teaching Catholic doctrine and, in particular, for formulating local catechisms. But it was also confirmed by its vast favourable reception in all segments of the People of God, who have come to know and appreciate it in more than fifty translations which to date have been published.

It is with great joy that I now approve and promulgate the *Compendium* of that *Catechism*.

The *Compendium* had been fervently desired by the participants in the International Catechetical Congress of October 2002, which gave voice to a need widely felt in the Church. My beloved Predecessor, recognising this desire, decided in February 2003 to begin preparation of the text by entrusting the work to a Commission of Cardinals, over which I presided, and which was assisted by various experts. In the course of the work, a draft of the *Compendium* was submitted to all the Cardinals and the Presidents of Conferences of Bishops, the vast majority of whom evaluated the text favourably.

The *Compendium*, which I now present to the Universal Church, is a faithful and sure synthesis of the *Catechism of the Catholic Church*. It contains, in concise form, all the essential and fundamental elements of the Church's faith, thus constituting, as my Predecessor had wished, a kind of *vademecum* which allows believers and non-believers alike to behold the entire panorama of the Catholic faith.

In its structure, contents and language, the *Compendium* faithfully reflects the *Catechism of the Catholic Church* and will thus assist in making the *Catechism* more widely known and more deeply understood.

I entrust this *Compendium* above all to the entire Church and, in particular, to every Christian, in order that it may awaken in the Church of the third millennium renewed zeal for evangelisation and education in the faith, which ought to characterise every community in the Church and every Christian believer, regardless of age or nationality.

But this *Compendium*, with its brevity, clarity and comprehensiveness, is directed to every human being, who, in a world of distractions and multifarious messages, desires to know the Way of Life, the Truth, entrusted by God to His Son's Church.

Through the intercession of Mary Most Holy, Mother of Christ and Mother of the Church, may everyone who reads this authoritative text recognise and embrace ever more fully the inexhaustible beauty, uniqueness and significance of the incomparable Gift which God has made to the human race in His only Son, Jesus Christ, the "Way, the Truth, and the Life" (*John* 14:6).

Given on 28 June 2005, the vigil of the Solemnity of the Holy Apostles Peter and Paul, in the first year of my Pontificate.

The icon of Christ the *Pantocrator* (he who rules all), of rare artistic beauty, calls to mind the words of the psalmist: "Fairer in beauty are you than the sons of men; grace is poured out upon your lips" (*Psalm* 45:3).

Saint John Chrysostom applied this praise to the Lord Jesus when he wrote: "The Christ was in the prime of life with the strength of the Spirit and there shone forth in him a twofold beauty, that of soul and body" (*PG* 52, 479).

With its figurative expression, this icon represents the synthesis of the first ecumenical councils by successfully portraying both the splendour of Jesus' humanity and the brilliance of his divinity.

Christ is clothed in a red tunic covered with a dark blue cloak. The two colours call to mind his twofold nature while the gold reflections call attention to the divine person of the Word. A golden stole, the symbol of his eternal priesthood, falls from his right shoulder. The face, majestic and serene, framed by a thick head of hair and surrounded by a cross-bearing halo conveying the Greek trilateral "O Ω N" ("He who is"), recalls the revelation of the name of God in Exodus 3:14. Above and at the sides of the icon, there are the two diliterals: "IC - XC" ("Jesus" - "Christ") which represent the title of the image itself.

The right hand, with thumb and ring finger curved to the point of touching each other (to signify the two natures of Christ in the unity of his person), is held in a typical gesture of blessing. The left hand instead holds fast to the book of the Gospel which is adorned with three clasps, pearls, and precious stones. The Gospel, symbol and synthesis of the Word of God, has also a liturgical significance since in the celebration of the Eucharist a passage from it is read and the very words of Jesus are pronounced at the the consecration.

This image, a sublime synthesis of natural and symbolic elements, is an invitation to contemplate and to follow the Lord. Jesus through the Church, his bride and his mystical body, still continues today to bless the human family and to shed light upon it with his Gospel which is the authentic book of truth, happiness, and salvation for man.

In August of 386 while in a garden, Augustine heard a voice saying "Take and read, take and read" (*Confessions*, 8,12,29). The *Compendium of the Catechism of the Catholic Church*, as a synthesis of the Gospel of Jesus taught by the Church's catechesis is an invitation to open the book of truth and to read it, even to devour it as did the prophet Ezekiel (cf. *Ezekiel* 3:1-4).

THEOPHANOS OF CRETE (1546), *The Icon of Christ*, Stavronikita Monastery (Mount Athos).

INTRODUCTION

1. On 11 October 1992, Pope John Paul II presented the *Catechism of the Catholic Church* to the faithful of the whole world, describing it as a "reference text"[1] for a catechesis renewed at the living sources of the faith. Thirty years after the opening of the Second Vatican Council (1962-1965), the desire for a catechism of all Catholic doctrine on faith and morals, which had been voiced in 1985 by the extraordinary Assembly of the Synod of Bishops, came to fulfilment.

Five years later, on 15 August 1997, the Pope promulgated the *editio typica* of the *Catechismus Catholicae Ecclesiae* and confirmed its fundamental purpose "as a full, complete exposition of Catholic doctrine, enabling everyone to know what the Church professes, celebrates, lives and prays in her daily life".[2]

2. In order to realise more fully the *Catechism's* potential and in response to the request that had emerged at the International Catechetical Congress of October 2002, Pope John Paul II, in 2003, established a Commission under the presidency of Cardinal Joseph Ratzinger, Prefect of the Congregation for the Doctrine of the Faith, which was given the task of drafting a *Compendium* of the *Catechism of the Catholic Church*, as a more concise formulation of its contents of faith. After two years of work, a *draft compendium* was prepared and distributed among the Cardinals and the Presidents of Conferences of Bishops for their consultation. The draft, as a whole, was evaluated positively in the great majority of the responses that were received. Therefore, the Commission proceeded to revise the draft and, taking account of the proposals for improvement that had been submitted, prepared the final text.

3. There are three principal characteristics of the *Compendium*: the close reliance on the *Catechism of the Catholic Church*; the dialogical format; the use of *artistic images* in the catechesis.

[1] John Paul II, Apostolic Constitution *Fidei depositum*, 11 October 1992.

[2] John Paul II, Apostolic Letter *Laetamur magnopere*, 15 August 1997.

The *Compendium* is not a work that stands alone, nor is it intended in any way to replace the *Catechism of the Catholic Church*: instead, it refers constantly to the *Catechism* by means of reference numbers printed in the margins, as well as by consistent reliance on its structure, development and contents. In fact, the *Compendium* is meant to reawaken interest in and enthusiasm for the *Catechism*, which, in the wisdom of its presentation and the depth of its spirituality, always remains the basic text for catechesis in the Church today.

Like the *Catechism*, the *Compendium* has four parts, corresponding to the fundamental laws of life in Christ.

The first part, entitled "The Profession of Faith", contains a synthesis of the *lex credendi*, the faith professed by the Catholic Church, as expressed in the Apostles' Creed which is further elaborated by the Nicene-Constantinopolitan Creed. In the liturgical profession of the Creed, the Christian assembly keeps the principal truths of the faith alive in memory.

The second part, entitled "The Celebration of the Christian Mystery", presents the essential elements of the *lex celebrandi*. The proclamation of the Gospel finds its authentic response in the sacramental life, through which Christians experience and witness, in every moment of their existence, the saving power of the paschal mystery by which Christ has accomplished our redemption.

The third part, entitled "Life in Christ", recalls the *lex vivendi*, through which the baptised manifest their commitment to the faith they have professed and celebrated, through their actions and ethical choices. The Christian faithful are called by the Lord Jesus to act in a way which befits their dignity as children of the Father in the charity of the Holy Spirit.

The fourth part, entitled "Christian Prayer", summarises the *lex orandi*, the life of prayer. Following the example of Jesus, the perfect model of one who prays, the Christian too is called to the dialogue with God in prayer. A privileged expression of prayer is the *Our Father*, the prayer that Jesus has taught us.

4. A second characteristic of the *Compendium* is its dialogical format, reflecting the ancient catechetical literary genre of questions and answers. The idea is to reproduce an imaginary dialogue between master and disciple, through a series of incisive questions that invite the reader to go deeper in discovering ever new aspects of his faith. The dialogical format also lends itself to brevity in the text, by reducing it to what is essential. This may help the reader to grasp the contents and possibly to memorise them as well.

5. A third characteristic is the inclusion of some artistic images which mark the elaboration of the *Compendium*. These are drawn from the rich patrimony of Christian iconography. The centuries-old conciliar tradition teaches us that images are also a preaching of the Gospel. Artists in every age have offered the principal facts of the mystery of salvation to the contemplation and wonder of believers by presenting them in the splendour of colour and in the perfection of beauty. It is an indication of how today more than ever, in a culture of images, a sacred image can express much more than what can be said in words, and be an extremely effective and dynamic way of communicating the Gospel message.

6. Forty years after the close of the Second Vatican Council and in the year of the Eucharist, this *Compendium* represents an additional resource for satisfying the hunger for truth among the Christian faithful of all ages and conditions, as well as the hunger for truth and justice among those who are without faith. The publication of the *Compendium* will take place on the solemnity of the Holy Apostles Peter and Paul, pillars of the Church universal and exemplary evangelisers of the ancient world. These apostles saw what they preached and witnessed to the truth of Christ even unto martyrdom. Let us imitate them in their missionary zeal and pray to the Lord that the Church may always follow the teaching of the apostles, from whom she first received the glorious proclamation of the faith.

20 March 2005, Palm Sunday.

✠ JOSEPH CARDINAL RATZINGER
President of the Special Commission

The Adoration of the Magi (cf. *Matthew* 2:1-12) is a splendid masterpiece which portrays the revelation of Jesus to all peoples. The Incarnation is a gift not only to the faith of Mary, Joseph, the women, the shepherds, and the simple folk of Israel but to the faith of these foreigners who came from the east to adore the newborn Messiah and offer him their gifts.

"On entering the house, they saw the child with Mary his mother. They prostrated themselves and did him homage. Then they opened their treasures and offered him gifts of gold, frankincense and myrrh" (*Matthew* 2:11).

The magi are the first fruits of the nations who are called to the faith and they approached Jesus not with empty hands but with the riches of their lands and cultures.

The Gospel of Jesus is the word of salvation for all humanity. Saint Leo the Great said: "Let all peoples, represented by the three magi, adore the Creator of the universe and may God be known not just in Judea but through all the earth because everywhere in Israel great is his name (cf. *Psalm* 75:2)" (*Discourse* 3 *for the Epiphany*).

The first part of the *Compendium* illustrates the encounter between God and man and the response of faith which the Church gives in the name of all people to the gift of the redeeming Incarnation of the Son of God and his divine revelation.

GENTILE DA FABRIANO (1423), *Adoration of the Magi*, Uffizi Gallery, Florence.

PART ONE

THE PROFESSION
OF FAITH

SECTION ONE

"I BELIEVE" - "WE BELIEVE"

This illumination presents the complete cycle of the six days of creation up to the temptation of our first parents (cf. *Genesis* 1-3).

"O Lord, how manifold are your works! In wisdom hast thou made them all; the earth is full of thy creatures. Yonder is the sea also, great and wide, which teems with things innumerable, living things both small and great. There go the ships, and Leviathan which thou didst form to sport in it. These all look to thee, to give them their food in due season. When thou givest to them, they gather it up; when thou openest thy hand, they are filled with good things... Bless the Lord, O my soul!" (*Psalm* 103:24-28,35).

The Church at the Easter vigil praises the Lord for the even more wonderful work of the redemption of mankind and the cosmos:

"Almighty and eternal God, you created all things
in wonderful beauty and order. Help us now to
perceive how still more wonderful is the new
creation by which in the fullness of time you
redeemed your people through the sacrifice of
our Passover, Jesus Christ."

───────────

BIBLE OF SOUVIGNY, *Illumination on the Days of Creation*, Moulins, Municipal Library.

1. What is the plan of God for man?

God, infinitely perfect and blessed in himself, in a plan of sheer goodness   1-25
freely created man to make him share in his own blessed life. In the fullness
of time, God the Father sent his Son as the Redeemer and Saviour of
mankind, fallen into sin, thus calling all into his Church and, through the
work of the Holy Spirit, making them adopted children and heirs of his
eternal happiness.

CHAPTER ONE

MAN'S CAPACITY FOR GOD

"You are great, O Lord, and greatly to be praised [...] You have made   30
us for yourself and our heart is restless until it rests in you."
(Saint Augustine)

2. Why does man have a desire for God?

God himself, in creating man in his own image, has written upon his   27-30
heart the desire to see him. Even if this desire is often ignored, God never   44-45
ceases to draw man to himself because only in God will he find and live the
fullness of truth and happiness for which he never stops searching. By
nature and by vocation, therefore, man is a religious being, capable of
entering into communion with God. This intimate and vital bond with God
confers on man his fundamental dignity.

3. How is it possible to know God with only the light of human reason?

Starting from creation, that is from the world and from the human   31-36
person, through reason alone one can know God with certainty as the origin   46-47
and end of the universe, as the highest good and as infinite truth and beauty.

4. Is the light of reason alone sufficient to know the mystery of God?

In coming to a knowledge of God by the light of reason alone man   37-38
experiences many difficulties. Indeed, on his own he is unable to enter into
the intimacy of the divine mystery. This is why he stands in need of being
enlightened by God's revelation, not only about those things that exceed his
understanding, but also about those religious and moral truths which of
themselves are not beyond the grasp of human reason, so that even in the
present condition of the human race, they can be known by all with ease,
with firm certainty and with no admixture of error.

5. How can we speak about God?

39-43   By taking as our starting point the perfections of man and of the other
48-49   creatures which are a reflection, albeit a limited one, of the infinite perfection
of God, we are able to speak about God with all people. We must, however,
continually purify our language insofar as it is image-bound and imperfect,
realising that we can never fully express the infinite mystery of God.

CHAPTER TWO
GOD COMES TO MEET MAN

THE REVELATION OF GOD

6. What does God reveal to man?

50-53   God in his goodness and wisdom reveals himself. With deeds and words,
68-69   he reveals himself and his plan of loving goodness which he decreed from
all eternity in Christ. According to this plan, all people by the grace of the
Holy Spirit are to share in the divine life as adopted "sons" in the only
begotten Son of God.

7. What are the first stages of God's Revelation?

54-58   From the very beginning, God manifested himself to our first parents,
70-71   Adam and Eve, and invited them to intimate communion with himself. After
their fall, he did not cease his revelation to them but promised salvation for
all their descendants. After the flood, he made a covenant with Noah, a
covenant between himself and all living beings.

8. What are the next stages of God's Revelation?

59-64   God chose Abram, calling him out of his country, making him "the father of
72   a multitude of nations" (*Genesis* 17:5), and promising to bless in him "all the
nations of the earth" (*Genesis* 12:3). The people descended from Abraham would
be the trustee of the divine promise made to the patriarchs. God formed Israel as
his chosen people, freeing them from slavery in Egypt, establishing with them
the covenant of Mount Sinai, and, through Moses, giving them his law. The
prophets proclaimed a radical redemption of the people and a salvation which
would include all nations in a new and everlasting covenant. From the people of
Israel and from the house of King David, would be born the Messiah, Jesus.

9. What is the full and definitive stage of God's Revelation?

65-66   The full and definitive stage of God's revelation is accomplished in his
73   Word made flesh, Jesus Christ, the mediator and fullness of Revelation. He,

being the only-begotten Son of God made man, is the perfect and definitive Word of the Father. In the sending of the Son and the gift of the Spirit, Revelation is now fully complete, although the faith of the Church must gradually grasp its full significance over the course of centuries.

> *"In giving us his Son, his only and definitive Word, God spoke everything to us at once in this sole Word, and he has no more to say."* (Saint John of the Cross)

10. What is the value of private revelations?

While not belonging to the deposit of faith, private revelations may help   67
a person to live the faith as long as they lead us to Christ. The Magisterium of the Church, which has the duty of evaluating such private revelations, cannot accept those which claim to surpass or correct that definitive Revelation which is Christ.

THE TRANSMISSION OF DIVINE REVELATION

11. Why and in what way is divine revelation transmitted?

God "desires all men to be saved and to come to the knowledge of the   74
truth" (1 *Timothy* 2:4), that is, of Jesus Christ. For this reason, Christ must be proclaimed to all according to his own command, "Go forth and teach all nations" (*Matthew* 28:19). And this is brought about by Apostolic Tradition.

12. What is Apostolic Tradition?

Apostolic Tradition is the transmission of the message of Christ, brought   75-79
about from the very beginnings of Christianity by means of preaching, bearing   83
witness, institutions, worship, and inspired writings. The apostles transmitted all   96, 98
they received from Christ and learned from the Holy Spirit to their successors, the bishops, and through them to all generations until the end of the world.

13. In what ways does Apostolic Tradition occur?

Apostolic Tradition occurs in two ways: through the living transmission   76
of the Word of God (also simply called Tradition) and through Sacred Scripture which is the same proclamation of salvation in written form.

14. What is the relationship between Tradition and Sacred Scripture?

Tradition and Sacred Scripture are bound closely together and   80-82
communicate one with the other. Each of them makes present and fruitful in   97
the Church the mystery of Christ. They flow out of the same divine well-

spring and together make up one sacred deposit of faith from which the Church derives her certainty about Revelation.

15. To whom is the deposit of faith entrusted?

84, 91   The apostles entrusted the deposit of faith to the whole of the Church.
94, 99 Thanks to its supernatural sense of faith the people of God as a whole, assisted by the Holy Spirit and guided by the Magisterium of the Church, never ceases to welcome, to penetrate more deeply and to live more fully from the gift of divine Revelation.

16. To whom is given the task of authentically interpreting the deposit of faith?

85-90   The task of giving an authentic interpretation of the deposit of faith has
100 been entrusted to the living teaching office of the Church alone, that is, to the successor of Peter, the bishop of Rome, and to the bishops in communion with him. To this Magisterium, which in the service of the Word of God enjoys the certain charism of truth, belongs also the task of defining dogmas which are formulations of the truths contained in divine Revelation. This authority of the Magisterium also extends to those truths necessarily connected with Revelation.

17. What is the relationship between Scripture, Tradition and the Magisterium?

95   Scripture, Tradition, and the Magisterium are so closely united with each other that one of them cannot stand without the others. Working together, each in its own way, under the action of the one Holy Spirit, they all contribute effectively to the salvation of souls.

SACRED SCRIPTURE

18. Why does Sacred Scripture teach the truth?

105-108   Because God himself is the author of Sacred Scripture. For this reason it
135-136 is said to be inspired and to teach without error those truths which are necessary for our salvation. The Holy Spirit inspired the human authors who wrote what he wanted to teach us. The Christian faith, however, is not a "religion of the Book", but of the Word of God - "not a written and mute word, but incarnate and living" (Saint Bernard of Clairvaux).

19. How is Sacred Scripture to be read?

109-119   Sacred Scripture must be read and interpreted with the help of the Holy
137 Spirit and under the guidance of the Magisterium of the Church according

to three criteria: 1) it must be read with attention to the content and unity of the whole of Scripture; 2) it must be read within the living Tradition of the Church; 3) it must be read with attention to the analogy of faith, that is, the inner harmony which exists among the truths of the faith themselves.

20. What is the *Canon* of Scripture?

The *Canon* of Scripture is the complete list of the sacred writings which the Church has come to recognise through Apostolic Tradition. The *Canon* consists of 46 books of the Old Testament and 27 of the New.

120
138

21. What is the importance of the Old Testament for Christians?

Christians venerate the Old Testament as the true Word of God. All of the books of the Old Testament are divinely inspired and retain a permanent value. They bear witness to the divine pedagogy of God's saving love. They are written, above all, to prepare for the coming of Christ the Saviour of the universe.

121-123

22. What importance does the New Testament have for Christians?

The New Testament, whose central object is Jesus Christ, conveys to us the ultimate truth of divine Revelation. Within the New Testament the four Gospels of Matthew, Mark, Luke and John are the heart of all the Scriptures because they are the principle witness to the life and teaching of Jesus. As such, they hold a unique place in the Church.

124-127
139

23. What is the unity that exists between the Old and the New Testaments?

Scripture is one insofar as the Word of God is one. God's plan of salvation is one, and the divine inspiration of both Testaments is one. The Old Testament prepares for the New and the New Testament fulfills the Old; the two shed light on each other.

128-130
140

24. What role does Sacred Scripture play in the life of the Church?

Sacred Scripture gives support and vigour to the life of the Church. For the children of the Church, it is a confirmation of the faith, food for the soul and the fount of the spiritual life. Sacred Scripture is the soul of theology and of pastoral preaching. The Psalmist says that it is "a lamp to my feet and a light to my path" (*Psalm* 119:105). The Church, therefore, exhorts all to read Sacred Scripture frequently because "ignorance of the Scriptures is ignorance of Christ" (Saint Jerome).

131-133
141

CHAPTER THREE

MAN'S RESPONSE TO GOD

I BELIEVE

25. How does man respond to God who reveals himself?

142-143   Sustained by divine grace, we respond to God with the obedience of faith, which means the full surrender of ourselves to God and the acceptance of his truth insofar as it is guaranteed by the One who is Truth itself.

26. Who are the principal witnesses of the obedience of faith in the Sacred Scriptures?

144-149   There are many such witnesses, two in particular: One is *Abraham* who when put to the test "believed in God" (*Romans* 4:3) and always obeyed his call. For this reason he is called "the Father of all who believe" (*Romans* 4:11-18). The other is the *Virgin Mary* who, throughout her entire life, embodied in a perfect way the obedience of faith: "*Let it be done to me according to your word*" (*Luke* 1:38).

27. What does it mean in practice for a person to believe in God?

150-152   It means to adhere to God himself, entrusting oneself to him and
176-178   giving assent to all the truths which God has revealed because God is Truth. It means to believe in one God in three Persons, Father, Son, and Holy Spirit.

28. What are the characteristics of faith?

153-165   Faith is the supernatural virtue which is *necessary* for salvation. It is
179-180   a *free gift* of God and is accessible to all who humbly seek it. The act of
183-184   faith is *a human act*, that is, an act of the intellect of a person - prompted by the will moved by God - who freely assents to divine truth. Faith is also *certain* because it is founded on the Word of God; it *works* "through charity" (*Galatians* 5:6); and it *continually grows* through listening to the Word of God and through prayer. It is, even now, a *foretaste* of the joys of heaven.

29. Why is there no contradiction between faith and science?

159   Though faith is above reason, there can never be a contradiction between faith and science because both originate in God. It is God himself who gives to us the light both of reason and of faith.

"I believe, in order to understand; and I understand, the better to believe." (Saint Augustine)

WE BELIEVE

30. Why is faith a personal act, and at the same time ecclesial?

Faith is a personal act insofar as it is the free response of the human person to God who reveals himself. But at the same time it is an ecclesial act which expresses itself in the proclamation, "We believe". It is in fact the Church that belicves: and thus by the grace of the Holy Spirit precedes, engenders and nourishes the faith of each Christian. For this reason the Church is Mother and Teacher. 166-169 181

"No one can have God as Father who does not have the Church as Mother." (Saint Cyprian)

31. Why are the formulas of faith important?

The formulas of faith are important because they permit one to express, assimilate, celebrate, and share together with others the truths of the faith through a common language. 170-171

32. In what way is the faith of the Church one faith alone?

The Church, although made up of persons who have diverse languages, cultures, and rites, nonetheless professes with a united voice the one faith that was received from the one Lord and that was passed on by the one Apostolic Tradition. She confesses one God alone, Father, Son, and Holy Spirit, and points to one way of salvation. Therefore we believe with one heart and one soul all that is contained in the Word of God, handed down or written, and which is proposed by the Church as divinely revealed. 172-175 182

SECTION TWO
THE PROFESSION
OF THE CHRISTIAN FAITH

This ancient mosaic found in the Roman basilica of Saint Clement celebrates the triumph of the cross, the central mystery of the Christian faith. One can observe the luxuriant embellishment of a tuft of acanthus leaves from which come forth so many circlets going out in all directions with their flowers and fruits. This plant takes its vitality from the cross of Jesus whose sacrifice is the re-creation of mankind and the cosmos. Jesus is the new Adam who by the mystery of his passion, death, and Resurrection brings about the rebirth of mankind and its reconciliation with the Father.

Around the suffering Christ are twelve white doves who represent the twelve apostles. At the foot of the cross are Mary and John, the beloved disciple:

"When Jesus saw his mother, and the disciple whom he loved standing near, he said to his mother, 'Woman, behold, your son!' Then he said to the disciple, 'Behold your mother!' And from that hour the disciple took her into his own home" (*John* 19:26-27).

Above the cross the Father's hand is extended, offering a crown of glory to his Son who by his paschal mystery is the victor over death.

At the base of the plant there is a little stag who does battle with the evil serpent.

From this plant which stands for the tree of redemption, there comes forth a spring of gushing water giving life to the four rivulets, symbols of the four gospels, at which the faithful quench their thirst like deer at the springs of living water. The Church is here pictured as a heavenly garden given life by Christ, the true tree of life.

BASILICA OF SAINT CLEMENT, *Mosaic in the Apse*, Rome.

THE CREED

The Apostles' Creed

I believe in God the Father almighty, creator of heaven and earth. And in Jesus Christ, His only Son, our Lord, who was conceived by the Holy Spirit, born of the Virgin Mary, suffered under Pontius Pilate, was crucified, died, and was buried. He descended into hell; on the third day He rose again from the dead; He ascended into heaven, and sits at the right hand of God the Father almighty; from thence He shall come to judge the living and the dead.

I believe in the Holy Spirit,
the holy Catholic Church,
the communion of saints,
the forgiveness of sins,
the resurrection of the body
and life everlasting.

Amen.

The Nicene-Constantinopolitan Creed

I believe in one God, the Father, the Almighty, maker of heaven and earth, of all that is, seen and unseen.

I believe in one Lord, Jesus Christ, the only Son of God, eternally begotten of the Father, God from God, Light from Light, true God from true God, begotten, not made, one in Being with the Father.

Symbolum Apostolicum

Credo in Deum Patrem omnipoténtem, Creatórem cæli et terræ, et in Iesum Christum, Fílium Eius únicum, Dóminum nostrum, qui concéptus est de Spíritu Sancto, natus ex María Vírgine, passus sub Póntio Piláto, crucifíxus, mórtuus, et sepúltus, descéndit ad ínferos, tértia die resurréxit a mórtuis, ascéndit ad cælos, sedet ad déxteram Dei Patris omnipoténtis, inde ventúrus est iudicáre vivos et mórtuos.

Et in Spíritum Sanctum,
sanctam Ecclésiam cathólicam,
sanctórum communiónem,
remissiónem peccatórum,
carnis resurrectiónem,
vitam ætérnam.

Amen.

Symbolum Nicænum Constantinopolitanum

Credo in unum Deum, Patrem omnipoténtem, Factórem cæli et terræ, visibílium ómnium et invisibílium.

Et in unum Dóminum Iesum Christum, Fílium Dei unigénitum et ex Patre natum ante ómnia sǽcula: Deum de Deo, Lumen de Lúmine, Deum verum de Deo vero, génitum, non factum, consub-stantiálem Patri:

Through Him all things were made. For us men and for our salvation, He came down from heaven: by the power of the Holy Spirit, He was born of the Virgin Mary, and became Man. For our sake He was crucified under Pontius Pilate; He suffered, died, and was buried. On the third day He rose again in fulfillment of the Scriptures; He ascended into heaven, and is seated at the right hand of the Father. He will come again in glory to judge the living and the dead, and His kingdom will have no end.

I believe in the Holy Spirit, the Lord, the Giver of life, who proceeds from the Father and the Son. With the Father and the Son He is worshipped and glorified. He has spoken through the prophets.

I believe in one, holy, catholic, and apostolic Church.

I acknowledge one Baptism for the forgiveness of sins. I look for the resurrection of the dead, and the life of the world to come.

Amen.

per quem ómnia facta sunt;
qui propter nos hómines
et propter nostram salútem,
descéndit de cælis, et incarnátus est
de Spíritu Sancto ex María Vírgine
et homo factus est, crucifíxus étiam
pro nobis sub Póntio Piláto, passus
et sepúltus est, et resurréxit tértia
die secúndum Scriptúras,
et ascéndit in cælum, sedet ad
déxteram Patris, et íterum ventúrus
est cum glória, iudicáre vivos et
mórtuos, cuius regni
non erit finis.

Credo in Spíritum Sanctum, Dóminum et vivificántem, qui ex Patre
Filióque procédit, qui cum Patre et
Fílio simul adorátur et conglorificá-
tur, qui locútus est per prophétas.

Et unam sanctam cathólicam
et apostólicam Ecclésiam.

Confíteor unum Baptísma
in remissiónem peccatórum.
Et exspécto resurrectiónem mor-
tuórum, et vitam ventúri sæculi.

Amen.

CHAPTER ONE
I BELIEVE IN GOD THE FATHER

The Symbols of Faith

33. What are the symbols of faith?

The symbols of faith are composite formulas, also called "professions of faith" or "Creeds", with which the Church from her very beginning has set forth synthetically and handed on her own faith in a language that is normative and common to all the faithful.

185-188
192, 197

34. What are the most ancient symbols (professions) of faith?

The most ancient symbols of faith are the *baptismal* creeds. Because Baptism is conferred "in the name of the Father, and of the Son, and of the Holy Spirit" (*Matthew* 28:19), the truths of faith professed at Baptism are articulated in reference to the three Persons of the Most Holy Trinity.

189-191

35. What are the most important symbols of the faith?

They are the *Apostles' Creed* which is the ancient baptismal symbol of the Church of Rome and the *Nicene-Constantinopolitan Creed* which stems from the first two ecumenical Councils, that of Nicea (325 A.D.) and that of Constantinople (381 A.D.) and which even to this day are common to all the great Churches of the East and the West.

193-195

"I BELIEVE IN GOD THE FATHER ALMIGHTY,
CREATOR OF HEAVEN AND EARTH."

36. Why does the Profession of Faith begin with the words, "I believe in God"?

The Profession of Faith begins with these words because the affirmation "I believe in God" is the most important, the source of all the other truths about man and about the world, and about the entire life of everyone who believes in God.

198-199

37. Why does one profess belief that there is only one God?

Belief in the one God is professed because he has revealed himself to the people of Israel as the only One when he said, "Hear, O Israel, the Lord our God is one Lord" (*Deuteronomy* 6:4) and "there is no other" (*Isaiah* 45:22). Jesus himself confirmed that God is "the one Lord" (*Mark* 12:29). To confess that Jesus and the Holy Spirit are also God and Lord does not introduce any division into the one God.

200-202
228

38. With what name does God reveal Himself?

203-209 God revealed himself to Moses as the living God, "the God of Abraham,
230-231 the God of Isaac, the God of Jacob" (*Exodus* 3:6). God also revealed to Moses
his mysterious name "I Am Who I Am (YHWH)". Already in Old Testament
times this ineffable name of God was replaced by the divine title *Lord*. Thus
in the New Testament, Jesus who was called *Lord* is seen as true God.

39. Is God the only One who "is"?

212-213 Since creatures have received everything they are and have from God,
only God in himself *is* the fullness of being and of every perfection. God is
"He who is" without origin and without end. Jesus also reveals that he bears
the divine name "I Am" (*John* 8:28).

40. Why is the revelation of God's name important?

206-213 In revealing his name, God makes known the riches contained in the
ineffable mystery of his being. He alone is from everlasting to everlasting.
He is the One who transcends the world and history. It is he who made
heaven and earth. He is the faithful God, always close to his people, in order
to save them. He is the highest holiness, "rich in mercy" (*Ephesians* 2:4),
always ready to forgive. He is the One who is spiritual, transcendent,
omnipotent, eternal, personal, and perfect. He is truth and love.

> *"God is the infinitely perfect being who is the most Holy Trinity."*
> (Saint Turibius of Montenegro)

41. In what way is God the truth?

214-217 God is Truth itself and as such he can neither deceive nor be deceived.
231 He is "light, and in him there is no darkness" (1 *John* 1:5). The eternal Son
of God, the incarnation of wisdom, was sent into the world "to bear witness
to the Truth" (*John* 18:37).

42. In what way does God reveal that he is love?

218-221 God revealed himself to Israel as the One who has a stronger love than
that of parents for their children or of husbands and wives for their spouses.
God in himself "is love" (1 *John* 4:8,16), who gives himself completely and
gratuitously, who "so loved the world that he gave his only Son so that the
world might be saved through him" (*John* 3:16-17). By sending his Son and
the Holy Spirit, God reveals that he himself is an eternal exchange of love.

43. What does it mean to believe in only one God?

To believe in the one and only God involves coming to know his   222-227
greatness and majesty. It involves living in thanksgiving and trusting always   229
in him, even in adversity. It involves knowing the unity and true dignity of
all human beings, created in his image. It involves making good use of the
things which he has created.

44. What is the central mystery of Christian faith and life?

The central mystery of Christian faith and life is the mystery of the Most   232-237
Blessed Trinity. Christians are baptised in the name of the Father and of the
Son and of the Holy Spirit.

45. Can the mystery of the Most Holy Trinity be known by the light of human reason alone?

God has left some traces of his trinitarian being in creation and in the Old   237
Testament but his inmost being as the Holy Trinity is a mystery which is
inaccessible to reason alone or even to Israel's faith before the Incarnation
of the Son of God and the sending of the Holy Spirit. This mystery was
revealed by Jesus Christ and it is the source of all the other mysteries.

46. What did Jesus Christ reveal to us about the mystery of the Father?

Jesus Christ revealed to us that God is "Father", not only insofar as he   240-242
created the universe and mankind, but above all because he eternally
generated in his bosom the Son who is his Word, "the radiance of the glory
of God and the very stamp of his nature" (*Hebrews* 1:3).

47. Who is the Holy Spirit revealed to us by Jesus Christ?

The Holy Spirit is the third Person of the Most Blessed Trinity. He is God,   243-248
one and equal with the Father and the Son. He "proceeds from the Father"
(*John* 15:26) who is the principle without a principle and the origin of all
trinitarian life. He proceeds also from the Son (*Filioque*) by the eternal Gift
which the Father makes of him to the Son. Sent by the Father and the Incarnate
Son, the Holy Spirit guides the Church "to know all truth" (*John* 16:13).

48. How does the Church express her trinitarian faith?

The Church expresses her trinitarian faith by professing a belief in the   249-256
oneness of God in whom there are three Persons: Father, Son, and Holy   266
Spirit. The three divine Persons are only one God because each of them
equally possesses the fullness of the one and indivisible divine nature.

They are really distinct from each other by reason of the relations which place them in correspondence to each other. The Father generates the Son; the Son is generated by the Father; the Holy Spirit proceeds from the Father and the Son.

49. How do the three divine Persons work?

257-260
267
Inseparable in their one substance, the three divine Persons are also inseparable in their activity. The Trinity has one operation, sole and the same. In this one divine action, however, each Person is present according to the mode which is proper to him in the Trinity.

> *"O my God, Trinity whom I adore... grant my soul peace; make it your heaven, your beloved dwelling, and the place of your rest. May I never abandon you there, but may I be there, whole and entire, completely vigilant in my faith, entirely adoring, and wholly given over to your creative action."* (Blessed Elizabeth of the Trinity)

50. What does it mean to say that God is almighty?

268-278
God reveals himself as "the strong One, the mighty One" (*Psalm* 24:8), as the One "to whom nothing is impossible" (*Luke* 1:37). His omnipotence is universal, mysterious and shows itself in the creation of the world out of nothing and humanity out of love; but above all it shows itself in the Incarnation and the Resurrection of his Son, in the gift of filial adoption and in the forgiveness of sins. For this reason, the Church directs her prayers to the "almighty and eternal God" (*"Omnipotens sempiterne Deus..."*).

51. What is the importance of affirming "In the beginning God created the heavens and the earth" (*Genesis* 1:1)?

279-289
315
The significance is that creation is the foundation of all God's saving plans. It shows forth the almighty and wise love of God, and it is the first step towards the covenant of the one God with his people. It is the beginning of the history of salvation which culminates in Christ; and it is the first answer to our fundamental questions regarding our very origin and destiny.

52. Who created the world?

290-292
316
The Father, the Son, and the Holy Spirit are the one and indivisible principle of creation even though the work of creating the world is particularly attributed to God the Father.

53. Why was the world created?

The world was created for the glory of God who wished to show forth   293-294
and communicate his goodness, truth and beauty. The ultimate end of   319
creation is that God, in Christ, might be "all in all" (1 *Corinthians* 15:28)
for his glory and for our happiness.

> "*The glory of God is man fully alive; moreover man's life is the vision of God.*" (Saint Irenaeus)

54. How did God create the universe?

God created the universe freely with wisdom and love. The world is not   295-301
the result of any necessity, nor of blind fate, nor of chance. God created "out   317-320
of nothing" (*ex nihilo*) (2 *Maccabees* 7:28) a world which is ordered and
good and which he infinitely transcends. God preserves his creation in being
and sustains it, giving it the capacity to act and leading it towards its
fulfillment through his Son and the Holy Spirit.

55. What is divine Providence?

Divine Providence consists in the dispositions with which God leads his   302-306
creatures towards their ultimate end. God is the sovereign Master of his own   321
plan. To carry it out, however, he also makes use of the cooperation of his
creatures. For God grants his creatures the dignity of acting on their own
and of being causes for each other.

56. How do we collaborate with divine Providence?

While respecting our freedom, God asks us to cooperate with him and gives   307-308
us the ability to do so through actions, prayers and sufferings, thus awakening   323
in us the desire "to will and to work for his good pleasure" (*Philippians* 2:13).

57. If God is omnipotent and provident, why then does evil exist?

To this question, as painful and mysterious as it is, only the *whole* of   309-310
Christian faith can constitute a response. God is not in any way - directly or   324, 400
indirectly - the cause of evil. He illuminates the mystery of evil in his Son
Jesus Christ who died and rose in order to vanquish that great moral evil,
human sin, which is at the root of all other evils.

58. Why does God permit evil?

Faith gives us the certainty that God would not permit evil if he did not   311-314
cause a good to come from that very evil. This was realised in a wondrous   324
way by God in the death and Resurrection of Christ. In fact, from the

greatest of all moral evils (the murder of his Son) he has brought forth the greatest of all goods (the glorification of Christ and our redemption).

Heaven and Earth

59. What did God create?

325-327 Sacred Scripture says, "In the beginning, God created the heavens and the earth" (*Genesis* 1:1). The Church in her profession of faith proclaims that God is the Creator of everything, visible and invisible, of all spiritual and corporeal beings, that is, of angels and of the visible world and, in a special way, of man.

60. Who are the angels?

328-333
350-351
The angels are purely spiritual creatures, incorporeal, invisible, immortal, and personal beings endowed with intelligence and will. They ceaselessly contemplate God face-to-face and they glorify him. They serve him and are his messengers in the accomplishment of his saving mission to all.

61. In what way are angels present in the life of the Church?

334-336
352
The Church joins with the angels in adoring God, invokes their assistance and commemorates some in her liturgy.

> *"Beside each believer stands an angel as a protector and shepherd leading him to life."* (Saint Basil the Great)

62. What does Sacred Scripture teach about the creation of the visible world?

337-344 Through the account of the "six days" of creation Sacred Scripture teaches us the value of the created world and its purpose, namely, to praise God and to serve humanity. Every single thing owes its very existence to God from whom it receives its goodness and perfection, its proper laws and its proper place in the universe.

63. What is the place of the human person in creation?

343-344
353
The human person is the summit of visible creation in as much as he or she is created in the image and likeness of God.

64. What kind of bond exists between created things?

342
354
There exists an interdependence and a hierarchy among creatures as willed by God. At the same time, there is also a unity and solidarity among

creatures since all have the same Creator, are loved by him and are ordered to his glory. Respecting the laws inscribed in creation and the relations which derive from the nature of things is, therefore, a principle of wisdom and a foundation for morality.

65. What is the relationship between the work of creation and the work of redemption?

The work of creation culminates in the still greater work of redemption, which in fact gives rise to a new creation in which everything will recover its true meaning and fulfillment.

345-349

Man

66. In what sense do we understand man and woman as created "in the image of God"?

The human person is created in the image of God in the sense that he or she is capable of knowing and of loving their Creator in freedom. Human beings are the only creatures on earth that God has willed for their own sake and has called to share, through knowledge and love, in his own divine life. All human beings, in as much as they are created in the image of God, have the dignity of a person. A person is not something but someone, capable of self-knowledge and of freely giving himself and entering into communion with God and with other persons.

355-357

67. For what purpose did God create man and woman?

God has created everything for them; but he has created them to know, serve and love God, to offer all of creation in this world in thanksgiving back to him and to be raised up to life with him in heaven. Only in the mystery of the incarnate Word does the mystery of the human person come into true light. Man and woman are predestined to reproduce the image of the Son of God made Man, who is the perfect "image of the invisible God" (*Colossians* 1:15).

358-359
380-381

68. Why does the human race form a unity?

All people form the unity of the human race by reason of the common origin which they have from God. God has made "from one ancestor all the nations of men" (*Acts* 17:26). All have but one Saviour and are called to share in the eternal happiness of God.

360-361

69. How do the soul and body form a unity in the human being?

The human person is a being at once corporeal and spiritual. In man spirit and matter form one nature. This unity is so profound that, thanks

362-365
382

to the spiritual principle which is the soul, the body which is material, becomes a living human body and participates in the dignity of the image of God.

70. Where does the soul come from?

366-368   The spiritual soul does not come from one's parents but is created
382   immediately by God and is immortal. It does not perish at the moment when it is separated from the body in death and it will be once again reunited with the body at the moment of the final resurrection.

71. What relationship has God established between man and woman?

369-373   Man and woman have been created by God in equal dignity insofar as
383   they are human persons. At the same time, they have been created in a reciprocal complementarity insofar as they are masculine and feminine. God has willed them one *for* the other to form a communion of persons. They are also called to transmit human life by forming in Matrimony "one flesh" (*Genesis* 2:24). They are likewise called to subdue the earth as "stewards" of God.

72. What was the original condition of the human person according to the plan of God?

374-379   In creating man and woman God had given them a special participation
384   in his own divine life in holiness and justice. In the plan of God they would not have had to suffer or die. Furthermore, a perfect harmony held sway within the human person, a harmony between creature and Creator, between man and woman, as well as between the first human couple and all of creation.

The Fall

73. How should we understand the reality of sin?

385-389   Sin is present in human history. This reality of sin can be understood clearly only in the light of divine Revelation and above all in the light of Christ the Saviour of all. Where sin abounded, he made grace abound all the more.

74. What was the fall of the angels?

391-395   This expression indicates that Satan and the other demons, about which
414   Sacred Scripture and the Tradition of the Church speak, were angels, created good by God. They were, however, transformed into evil because with a free and irrevocable choice they rejected God and his Kingdom, thus giving rise to the existence of hell. They try to associate human

beings with their revolt against God. However, God has wrought in Christ a sure victory over the Evil One.

75. What was the first human sin?

When tempted by the devil, the first man and woman allowed trust in their Creator to die in their hearts. In their disobedience they wished to become "like God" but without God and not in accordance with God (*Genesis* 3:5). Thus, Adam and Eve immediately lost for themselves and for all their descendants the original grace of holiness and justice. 396-403 415-417

76. What is original sin?

Original sin, in which all human beings are born, is the state of deprivation of original holiness and justice. It is a sin "contracted" by us not "committed"; it is a state of birth and not a personal act. Because of the original unity of all human beings, it is transmitted to the descendants of Adam "not by imitation, but by propagation". This transmission remains a mystery which we cannot fully understand. 404 419

77. What other consequences derive from original sin?

In consequence of original sin human nature, without being totally corrupted, is wounded in its natural powers. It is subject to ignorance, to suffering, and to the dominion of death and is inclined towards sin. This inclination is called *concupiscence*. 405-409 418

78. After the first sin, what did God do?

After the first sin the world was inundated with sin but God did not abandon man to the power of death. Rather, he foretold in a mysterious way in the "Protoevangelium" (*Genesis* 3:15) that evil would be conquered and that man would be lifted up from his fall. This was the first proclamation of the Messiah and Redeemer. Therefore, the fall would be called in the future a "*happy fault*" because it "gained for us so great a Redeemer" (Liturgy of the Easter Vigil). 410-412 420

CHAPTER TWO
I BELIEVE IN JESUS CHRIST
THE ONLY SON OF GOD

79. What is the Good News for humanity?

It is the proclamation of Jesus Christ, the "Son of the living God" (*Matthew* 16:16), who died and rose from the dead. In the time of King 422-424

Herod and the Emperor Caesar Augustus, God fulfilled the promises that he made to Abraham and his descendants. He sent "his Son, born of a woman, born under the law, to redeem those who were under the law, so that we might receive adoption as sons" (*Galatians* 4:4-5).

80. How is the Good News spread?

425-429   From the very beginning the first disciples burned with the desire to proclaim Jesus Christ in order to lead all to faith in him. Even today, from the loving knowledge of Christ there springs up in the believer the desire to evangelise and catechise, that is, to reveal in the Person of Christ the entire design of God and to put humanity in communion with him.

"AND IN JESUS CHRIST, HIS ONLY SON OUR LORD"

81. What is the meaning of the name "Jesus"?

430-435   Given by the angel at the time of the Annunciation, the name "Jesus"
452   means "God saves". The name expresses his identity and his mission "because he will save his people from their sins" (*Matthew* 1:21). Peter proclaimed that "there is no other name under heaven given to men by which we can be saved" (*Acts* 4:12).

82. Why is Jesus called "Christ"?

436-440   "Christ" in Greek, "Messiah" in Hebrew, means the "anointed one".
453   Jesus is the Christ because he is consecrated by God and anointed by the Holy Spirit for his redeeming mission. He is the Messiah awaited by Israel, sent into the world by the Father. Jesus accepted the title of Messiah but he made the meaning of the term clear: "come down from heaven" (*John* 3:13), crucified and then risen, he is the Suffering Servant "who gives his life as a ransom for the many" (*Matthew* 20:28). From the name Christ comes our name of *Christian*.

83. In what sense is Jesus the Only Begotten Son of God?

441-445   Jesus is the Son of God in a unique and perfect way. At the time of his
454   Baptism and his Transfiguration, the voice of the Father designated Jesus as his "beloved Son". In presenting himself as the Son who "knows the Father" (*Matthew* 11:27), Jesus affirmed his singular and eternal relationship with God his Father. He is "the Only Begotten Son of God" (1 *John* 4:9), the second Person of the Blessed Trinity. He is the central figure of apostolic preaching. The apostles saw "his glory as of the Only Begotten of the Father" (*John* 1:14).

84. What is the meaning of the title "Lord"?

In the Bible this title regularly designates God as Sovereign. Jesus ascribed this title to himself and revealed his divine sovereignty by his power over nature, over demons, over sin, and over death, above all by his own Resurrection. The first Christian creeds proclaimed that the power, the honour, and the glory that are due to God the Father also belong to Jesus: God "has given him the name which is above every other name" (*Philippians* 2:9). He is the Lord of the world and of history, the only One to whom we must completely submit our personal freedom.   446-451 455

"JESUS CHRIST WAS CONCEIVED BY THE POWER OF THE HOLY SPIRIT, AND WAS BORN OF THE VIRGIN MARY"

85. Why did the Son of God become man?

For us men and for our salvation, the Son of God became incarnate in the womb of the Virgin Mary by the power of the Holy Spirit. He did so to reconcile us sinners with God, to have us learn of God's infinite love, to be our model of holiness and to make us "partakers of the divine nature" (2 *Peter* 1:4).   456-460

86. What does the word "Incarnation" mean?

The Church calls the mystery of the wonderful union of the divine and human natures in the one divine Person of the Word the "Incarnation". To bring about our salvation the Son of God was made "flesh" (*John* 1:14) and became truly man. Faith in the Incarnation is a distinctive sign of the Christian faith.   461-463 483

87. In what way is Jesus Christ true God and true man?

Jesus is inseparably true God and true man in the unity of his divine Person. As the Son of God, who is "begotten, not made, consubstantial with the Father," he was made true man, our brother, without ceasing to be God, our Lord.   464-467 469

88. What does the Council of Chalcedon (in the year 451) teach in this regard?

The Council of Chalcedon teaches us to confess "one and the same Son, our Lord Jesus Christ, perfect in his humanity, true God and true man, composed of rational soul and body, consubstantial with the Father by his divinity, and consubstantial with us by his humanity, 'like us in all things but sin' (*Hebrews* 4:15), begotten from the Father before all ages as to his divinity, and in these last days, for us and for our salvation, born of Mary, the Virgin and Mother of God, as to his humanity."   467

89. How does the Church set forth the Mystery of the Incarnation?

464-470   The Church confesses that Jesus Christ is true God and true man, with two
479-481   natures, a divine nature and a human nature, not confused with each other but
united in the Person of the Word. Therefore, in the humanity of Jesus all
things - his miracles, his suffering, and his death - must be attributed to his
divine Person which acts by means of his assumed human nature.

> *"O Only-begotten Son and Word of God, you who are immortal, you
> who deigned for our salvation to become incarnate of the holy
> Mother of God and ever Virgin Mary (...) You who are one of the Holy
> Trinity, glorified with the Father and the Holy Spirit, save us!"*
> (Byzantine Liturgy of Saint John Chrysostom)

90. Did the incarnate Son of God have a soul with human knowledge?

470-474   The Son of God assumed a body animated by a rational human soul.
482   With his human intellect Jesus learned many things by way of experience;
but also as man the Son of God had an intimate and immediate knowledge
of God his Father. He likewise understood people's secret thoughts and he
knew fully the eternal plans which he had come to reveal.

91. How did the two wills of the incarnate Word cooperate?

475   Jesus had a divine will and a human will. In his earthly life the Son of God
482   humanly willed all that he had divinely decided with the Father and the Holy
Spirit for our salvation. The human will of Christ followed without opposition
or reluctance the divine will or, in other words, it was subject to it.

92. Did Christ have a true human body?

476-477   Christ assumed a true human body by means of which the invisible God
became visible. This is the reason why Christ can be represented and
venerated in sacred images.

93. What does the heart of Jesus exemplify?

478   Jesus knew us and loved us with a human heart. His Heart, pierced for
our salvation, is the symbol of that infinite love with which he loves the
Father and each one of us.

94. What is the meaning of the expression "conceived by the power of the Holy Spirit..."?

484-486   This expression means that the Virgin Mary conceived the eternal Son
in her womb by the power of the Holy Spirit without the cooperation of a

man. The angel told her at the Annunciation that "the Holy Spirit will come upon you" (*Luke* 1:35).

95. "...Born of the Virgin Mary": Why is Mary truly the Mother of God?

Mary is truly the *Mother of God* because she is the Mother of Jesus (*John* 2:1;19:25). The One who was conceived by the power of the Holy Spirit and became truly her Son is actually the eternal Son of God the Father. He is God himself.

495
509

96. What does the "Immaculate Conception" mean?

God freely chose Mary from all eternity to be the Mother of his Son. In order to carry out her mission she herself was *conceived immaculate*. This means that, thanks to the grace of God and in anticipation of the merits of Jesus Christ, Mary was preserved from original sin from the first instant of her conception.

487-492
508

97. How does Mary cooperate in the divine plan of salvation?

By the grace of God Mary was kept free from every personal sin her whole life long. She is the one who is "full of grace" (*Luke* 1:28), "the all holy". When the angel announced to her that she would give birth to "the Son of the Most High" (*Luke* 1:32), she freely gave her consent with "the obedience of faith" (*Romans* 1:5). Mary thus gave herself entirely to the person and work of her Son Jesus, espousing wholeheartedly the divine will regarding salvation.

493-494
508-511

98. What does the virginal conception of Jesus mean?

The virginal conception of Jesus means that Jesus was conceived in the womb of the Virgin solely by the power of the Holy Spirit without the intervention of a man. He is the Son of the heavenly Father according to his divine nature and the Son of Mary according to his human nature. He is, however, truly the Son of God in both natures since there is in him only one Person who is divine.

496-498
503

99. In what sense is Mary "ever Virgin"?

Mary is ever virgin in the sense that she "remained a virgin in conceiving her Son, a virgin in giving birth to him, a virgin in carrying him, a virgin in nursing him at her breast, always a virgin" (Saint Augustine). Therefore, when the Gospels speak of the "brothers and sisters of Jesus", they are talking about the close relations of Jesus, according to the way of speaking used in Sacred Scripture.

499-507
510-511

100. In what way is the spiritual motherhood of Mary universal?

501-507   Mary had only one Son, Jesus, but in him her spiritual motherhood
511   extends to all whom he came to save. Obediently standing at the side of the
new Adam, Jesus Christ, the Virgin is the *new Eve*, the true mother of all the
living, who with a mother's love cooperates in their birth and their formation
in the order of grace. Virgin and Mother, Mary is the figure of the Church,
its most perfect realisation.

101. In what sense is the life of Christ a Mystery?

512-521   The entire life of Christ is a revelation. What was visible in the earthly
561-562   life of Jesus leads us to the *invisible mystery of his divine sonship*: "whoever
has seen me has seen the Father" (*John* 14:9). Furthermore, even though
salvation comes completely from the cross and the Resurrection, the entire
life of Christ is a *mystery of redemption* because everything that Jesus did,
said, and suffered had for its aim the salvation of fallen human beings and
the restoration of their vocation as children of God.

102. How did God prepare the world for the mystery of Christ?

522-524   God prepared for the coming of his Son over the centuries. He awakened in
the hearts of the pagans a dim expectation of this coming and he prepared for
it specifically through the Old Testament, culminating with *John the Baptist*
who was the last and greatest of the prophets. We relive this long period of
expectancy in the annual liturgical celebration of the season of Advent.

103. What does the Gospel teach about the mysteries of the birth and infancy of Jesus?

525-530   At *Christmas* the glory of heaven is shown forth in the weakness of a
563-564   baby; the *circumcision* of Jesus is a sign of his belonging to the Hebrew
people and is a prefiguration of our Baptism; the *Epiphany* is the
manifestation of the Messiah King of Israel to all the nations; at the
presentation in the temple, Simeon and Anna symbolise all the
anticipation of Israel awaiting its encounter with its Saviour; the *flight
into Egypt* and the massacre of the innocents proclaim that the entire life
of Christ will be under the sign of persecution; the *departure from Egypt*
recalls the exodus and presents Jesus as the new Moses and the true and
definitive liberator.

104. What does the hidden life of Jesus in Nazareth teach us?

533-534   In the course of his *hidden life* in Nazareth Jesus stayed in the silence
564   of an ordinary existence. This allows us to enter into fellowship with him

in the holiness to be found in a daily life marked by prayer, simplicity, work and family love. His obedience to Mary and to Joseph, his foster father, is an image of his filial obedience to the Father. Mary and Joseph accepted with faith the mystery of Jesus even though they did not always understand it.

105. Why did Jesus receive from John the "baptism of repentance for the forgiveness of sins" (*Luke* 3:3)?

To inaugurate his public life and to anticipate the "Baptism" of his death, he who was without sin accepted to be numbered among sinners. He was "the Lamb of God who takes away the sin of the world" (*John* 1:29). The Father proclaimed him to be "his beloved Son" (*Matthew* 3:17) and the Spirit descended upon him. The baptism of Jesus is a prefiguring of our baptism.

535-537
565

106. What do we learn from the temptations of Jesus in the desert?

The temptations of Jesus in the desert recapitulate the temptation of Adam in Paradise and the temptations of Israel in the desert. Satan tempts Jesus in regard to his obedience to the mission given him by the Father. Christ, the new Adam, resists and his victory proclaims that of his passion which is the supreme obedience of his filial love. The Church unites herself to this mystery in a special way in the liturgical season of *Lent*.

538-540
566

107. Who is invited to come into the Kingdom of God proclaimed and brought about by Jesus?

All are invited by Jesus to enter the Kingdom of God. Even the worst of sinners is called to convert and to accept the boundless mercy of the Father. Already here on earth, the Kingdom belongs to those who accept it with a humble heart. To them the mysteries of the Kingdom are revealed.

541-546
567

108. Why did Jesus manifest the Kingdom by means of signs and miracles?

Jesus accompanied his words with *signs* and *miracles* to bear witness to the fact that the Kingdom is present in him, the Messiah. Although he healed some people, he did not come to abolish all evils here below but rather to free us especially from the slavery of sin. The driving out of demons proclaimed that his cross would be victorious over "the ruler of this world" (*John* 12:31).

547-550
567

109. In the Kingdom, what authority did Jesus bestow upon his Apostles?

551-553   Jesus chose the *Twelve*, the future witnesses of his Resurrection, and made
567   them sharers of his mission and of his authority to teach, to absolve from sins,
and to build up and govern the Church. In this college, Peter received "the
keys of the Kingdom" (*Matthew* 16:19) and assumed the first place with the
mission to keep the faith in its integrity and to strengthen his brothers.

110. What is the meaning of the Transfiguration?

554-556   Above all the Transfiguration shows forth the Trinity: "the Father in the
568   voice, the Son in the man Jesus, the Spirit in the shining cloud" (Saint
Thomas Aquinas). Speaking with Moses and Elijah about his "departure"
(*Luke* 9:31), Jesus reveals that his glory comes by way of the cross and he
anticipates his resurrection and his glorious coming "which will change our
lowly body to be like his glorious body" (*Philippians* 3:21).

> *"You were transfigured on the mountain and your disciples, as much
> as they were capable of it, beheld your glory, O Christ our God, so
> that when they should see you crucified they would understand that
> your passion was voluntary, and proclaim to the world that you truly
> are the splendour of the Father."* (Byzantine Liturgy)

111. How did the messianic entrance into Jerusalem come about?

557-560   At the established time Jesus chose to go up to Jerusalem to suffer his
569-570   passion and death, and to rise from the dead. As the Messiah King who
shows forth the coming of the Kingdom, he entered into his city mounted
on a donkey. He was acclaimed by the little children whose shout of
joyful praise is taken up in the *Sanctus* of the Eucharistic liturgy:
"Blessed is He who comes in the name of the Lord! *Hosanna* (save us!)"
(*Matthew* 21:9). The liturgy of the Church opens Holy Week by
celebrating this entry into Jerusalem.

"JESUS CHRIST SUFFERED UNDER PONTIUS PILATE,
WAS CRUCIFIED, DIED AND WAS BURIED."

112. What is the importance of the Paschal Mystery of Jesus?

571-573   The Paschal Mystery of Jesus, which comprises his passion, death,
Resurrection, and glorification, stands at the centre of the Christian faith
because God's saving plan was accomplished once for all by the redemptive
death of his Son Jesus Christ.

113. What were the accusations by which Jesus was condemned to death?

Some of the leaders of Israel accused Jesus of acting against the law, the temple in Jerusalem, and in particular against faith in the one God because he proclaimed himself to be the Son of God. For this reason they handed him over to Pilate so that he might condemn him to death.

574-576

114. How did Jesus conduct himself in regard to the Law of Israel?

Jesus did not abolish the Law given by God to Moses on Mount Sinai but he fulfilled it by giving it its definitive interpretation. He himself was the divine Legislator who fully carried out this Law. Furthermore, as the faithful Servant, he offered by means of his expiatory death the only sacrifice capable of making atonement for all the "transgressions committed by men under the first Covenant" (*Hebrews* 9:15).

577-582 592

115. What was the attitude of Jesus towards the temple in Jerusalem?

Jesus was accused of hostility to the temple. On the contrary, he venerated it as "the house of his Father" (*John* 2:16); and it was there that he imparted an important part of his teaching. However, he also foretold its destruction in connection with his own death and he presented himself as the definitive dwelling place of God among men.

583-586 593

116. Did Jesus contradict Israel's faith in the one God and saviour?

Jesus never contradicted faith in the one God, not even when he performed the stupendous divine work which fulfilled the messianic promises and revealed himself as equal to God, namely the pardoning of sins. However, the call of Jesus to believe in him and to be converted makes it possible to understand the tragic misunderstanding of the Sanhedrin which judged Jesus to be worthy of death as a blasphemer.

587-591 594

117. Who is responsible for the death of Jesus?

The passion and death of Jesus cannot be imputed indiscriminately either to all the Jews that were living at that time or to their descendants. Every single sinner, that is, every human being is really the cause and the instrument of the sufferings of the Redeemer; and the greater blame in this respect falls on those above all who are Christians and who the more often fall into sin or delight in their vices.

595-598

118. Why was the death of Jesus part of God's plan?

599-605   To reconcile to himself all who were destined to die because of sin God
619   took the loving initiative of sending his Son that he might give himself up
for sinners. Proclaimed in the Old Testament, especially as the sacrifice of
the Suffering Servant, the death of Jesus came about "in accordance with
the Scriptures".

119. In what way did Christ offer himself to the Father?

606-609   The entire life of Christ was a free offering to the Father to carry out his
620   plan of salvation. He gave "his life as a ransom for many" (*Mark* 10:45) and
in this way he reconciled all of humanity with God. His suffering and death
showed how his humanity was the free and perfect instrument of that divine
love which desires the salvation of all people.

120. How is Jesus' offering expressed at the Last Supper?

610-611   At the Last Supper with his apostles on the eve of his passion Jesus
621   anticipated, that is, both symbolised his free self-offering and made it really
present: "This is my Body which *is given* for you" (*Luke* 22:19), "This is my
Blood which *is poured out*..." (*Matthew* 26:28) Thus he both instituted the
Eucharist as the "memorial" (1 *Corinthians* 11:25) of his sacrifice and
instituted his apostles as priests of the New Covenant.

121. What happened in the Agony in the Garden of Gethsemane?

612   Despite the horror which death represented for the sacred humanity of
Jesus "who is the Author of Life" (*Acts* 3:15), the human will of the Son of
God remained faithful to the will of the Father for our salvation. Jesus
accepted the duty to carry our sins in his Body "becoming obedient unto
death" (*Philippians* 2:8).

122. What are the results of the sacrifice of Christ on the cross?

613-617   Jesus freely offered his life as an expiatory sacrifice, that is, he made
622-623   reparation for our sins with the full obedience of his love unto death. This
love "to the end" (*John* 13:1) of the Son of God reconciled all of humanity
with the Father. The paschal sacrifice of Christ, therefore, redeems
humanity in a way that is unique, perfect, and definitive; and it opens up for
them communion with God.

123. Why does Jesus call upon his disciples to take up their cross?

618   By calling his disciples to take up their cross and follow him Jesus desires to
associate with his redeeming sacrifice those who are to be its first beneficiaries.

124. In what condition was the body of Christ while it lay in the tomb?

Christ underwent a real death and a true burial. However, the power of God preserved his body from corruption. 624-630

"JESUS CHRIST DESCENDED INTO HELL;
ON THE THIRD DAY HE ROSE AGAIN FROM THE DEAD."

125. What is the "hell" into which Jesus descended?

This "hell" was different from the *hell* of the damned. It was the state of all those, righteous and evil, who died before Christ. With his soul united to his divine Person Jesus went down to the just in hell who were awaiting their Redeemer so they could enter at last into the vision of God. When he had conquered by his death both death and the devil "who has the power of death" (*Hebrews* 2:14), he freed the just who looked forward to the Redeemer and opened for them the gates of heaven. 632-637

126. What place does the Resurrection of Christ occupy in our faith?

The Resurrection of Jesus is the crowning truth of our faith in Christ and represents along with his cross an essential part of the Paschal Mystery. 631, 638

127. What are the signs that bear witness to the Resurrection of Jesus?

Along with the essential sign of the empty tomb, the Resurrection of Jesus is witnessed to by the women who first encountered Christ and proclaimed him to the apostles. Jesus then "appeared to Cephas (Peter) and then to the Twelve. Following that he appeared to more than five hundred of the brethren at one time" (1 *Corinthians* 15:5-6) and to others as well. The apostles could not have invented the story of the Resurrection since it seemed impossible to them. As a matter of fact, Jesus himself upbraided them for their unbelief. 639-644 656-657

128. Why is the Resurrection at the same time a transcendent occurrence?

While being an historical event, verifiable and attested by signs and testimonies, the Resurrection, insofar as it is the entrance of Christ's humanity into the glory of God, transcends and surpasses history as a mystery of faith. For this reason the risen Christ did not manifest himself to the world but to his disciples, making them his witnesses to the people. 647 656-657

129. What is the condition of the risen body of Jesus?

645-646   The Resurrection of Christ was not a return to earthly life. His risen body is that which was crucified and bears the marks of his passion. However it also participates in the divine life, with the characteristics of a glorified body. Because of this the risen Jesus was utterly free to appear to his disciples how and where he wished and under various aspects.

130. How is the Resurrection the work of the Most Holy Trinity?

648-650   The Resurrection of Christ is a transcendent work of God. The three Persons act together according to what is proper to them: the Father manifests his power; the Son "takes again" the life which he freely offered (*John* 10:17), reuniting his soul and his body which the Spirit brings to life and glorifies.

131. What is the saving meaning of the Resurrection?

651-655   The Resurrection is the climax of the Incarnation. It confirms the divinity
    658   of Christ and all the things which he did and taught. It fulfills all the divine promises made for us. Furthermore the risen Christ, the conqueror of sin and death, is the principle of our justification and our resurrection. It procures for us now the grace of filial adoption which is a real share in the life of the only begotten Son. At the end of time he will raise up our bodies.

"Jesus Ascended into Heaven and is seated
at the right hand of God the Father almighty"

132. What does the Ascension mean?

659-667   After forty days during which Jesus showed himself to the apostles with ordinary human features which veiled his glory as the Risen One, Christ ascended into heaven and was seated at the right hand of the Father. He is the Lord who now in his humanity reigns in the everlasting glory of the Son of God and constantly intercedes for us before the Father. He sends us his Spirit and he gives us the hope of one day reaching the place he has prepared for us.

"From thence he shall come to judge the living and the dead"

133. How does the Lord Jesus now reign?

668-674   As the Lord of the cosmos and of history, the Head of his Church, the
    680   glorified Christ mysteriously remains on earth where his kingdom is already present in seed and in its beginning in the Church. One day he will return in glory but we do not know the time. Because of this we live in watchful anticipation, praying "Come, Lord" (*Revelation* 22:20).

134. How will the coming of the Lord in glory happen?

After the final cosmic upheaval of this passing world the glorious coming of Christ will take place. Then will come the definitive triumph of God in the parousia and the Last Judgment. Thus the Kingdom of God will be realised.

675-677
680

135. How will Christ judge the living and the dead?

Christ will judge with the power he has gained as the Redeemer of the world who came to bring salvation to all. The secrets of hearts will be brought to light as well as the conduct of each one towards God and towards his neighbour. Everyone, according to how he has lived, will either be filled with life or damned for eternity. In this way, "the fullness of Christ" (*Ephesians* 4:13) will come about in which "God will be all in all" (1 *Corinthians* 15:28).

678-679
681-682

CHAPTER THREE
I BELIEVE IN THE HOLY SPIRIT

"I BELIEVE IN THE HOLY SPIRIT"

136. What does the Church mean when she confesses: "I believe in the Holy Spirit"?

To believe in the Holy Spirit is to profess faith in the Third Person of the Most Holy Trinity who proceeds from the Father and the Son and "is worshipped and glorified with the Father and the Son". The Spirit is "sent into our hearts" (*Galatians* 4:6) so that we might receive new life as sons of God.

683-686

137. Why are the missions of the Son and the Holy Spirit inseparable?

In the indivisible Trinity, the Son and the Spirit are distinct but inseparable. From the very beginning until the end of time, when the Father sends his Son he also sends his Spirit who unites us to Christ in faith so that as adopted sons we can call God "Father" (*Romans* 8:15). The Spirit is invisible but we know him through his actions, when he reveals the Word to us and when he acts in the Church.

687-690
742-743

138. What are the names of the Holy Spirit?

"The Holy Spirit" is the proper name of the third Person of the Most Holy Trinity. Jesus also called him the Paraclete (Consoler or Advocate) and the Spirit of Truth. The New Testament also refers to him as the Spirit of Christ, of the Lord, of God - the Spirit of Glory and the Spirit of the Promise.

691-693

139. What symbols are used to represent the Holy Spirit?

694-701   There are many symbols of the Holy Spirit: *living water* which springs
from the wounded Heart of Christ and which quenches the thirst of the
baptised; *anointing* with oil, which is the sacramental sign of Confirmation;
fire which transforms what it touches; the *cloud*, dark or luminous, in which
the divine glory is revealed; the *imposition of hands* by which the Holy
Spirit is given; the *dove* which descended on Christ at his baptism and
remained with him.

140. What does it mean that the Spirit "has spoken through the prophets"?

687-688   The term "*prophets*" means those who were inspired by the Holy Spirit
702-716 to speak in the name of God. The Spirit brings the prophecies of the Old
743 Testament to their complete fulfillment in Christ whose mystery he reveals
in the New Testament.

141. What did the Holy Spirit accomplish in John the Baptist?

717-720   The Spirit filled John the Baptist, who was the last prophet of the Old
Testament. Under his inspiration John was sent to "prepare for the Lord a
people well disposed" (*Luke* 1:17). He was to proclaim the coming of
Christ, the Son of God, upon whom he saw the Spirit descend and remain,
the one who "baptises with the Spirit" (*John* 1:33).

142. What is the work of the Spirit in Mary?

721-726   The Holy Spirit brought to fulfillment in Mary all the waiting and the
744 preparation of the Old Testament for the coming of Christ. In a singular way
he filled her with grace and made her virginity fruitful so that she could give
birth to the Son of God made flesh. He made her the Mother of the "whole
Christ", that is, of Jesus the Head and of the Church his body. Mary was
present with the Twelve on the day of Pentecost when the Holy Spirit
inaugurated the "last days" with the manifestation of the Church.

143. What is the relationship between the Spirit and Christ Jesus in his earthly mission?

727-730   Beginning with his Incarnation, the Son of God was consecrated in his
745-746 humanity as the Messiah by means of the anointing of the Spirit. He
revealed the Spirit in his teaching, fulfilled the promises made to the
Fathers, and bestowed him upon the Church at its birth when he breathed on
the apostles after the Resurrection.

144. What happened at Pentecost?

Fifty days after the Resurrection at Pentecost the glorified Jesus Christ poured out the Spirit in abundance and revealed him as a divine Person so that the Holy Trinity was fully manifest. The mission of Christ and of the Spirit became the mission of the Church which is sent to proclaim and spread the mystery of the communion of the Holy Trinity.

731-732
738

> *"We have seen the true Light, we have received the heavenly Spirit, we have found the true faith: we adore the indivisible Trinity, who has saved us."* (Byzantine Liturgy, Troparion of Vespers of Pentecost)

145. What does the Spirit do in the Church?

The Spirit builds, animates and sanctifies the Church. As the Spirit of Love, he restores to the baptised the divine likeness that was lost through sin and causes them to live in Christ the very life of the Holy Trinity. He sends them forth to bear witness to the Truth of Christ and he organises them in their respective functions so that all might bear "the fruit of the Spirit" (*Galatians* 5:22).

733-741
747

146. How do Christ and his Spirit act in the hearts of the faithful?

Christ communicates his Spirit and the grace of God through the *sacraments* to all the members of the Church, who thus bear the fruits of the *new life* of the Spirit. The Holy Spirit is also the Master of *prayer*.

738-741

"I BELIEVE IN THE HOLY CATHOLIC CHURCH"

The Church in the Plan of God

147. What does the word *Church* mean?

The word *Church* refers to the people whom God calls and gathers together from every part of the earth. They form the assembly of those who through faith and Baptism have become children of God, members of Christ, and temples of the Holy Spirit.

751-752
777, 804

148. Are there other names and images with which the Bible speaks about the Church?

In Sacred Scripture we find many images which bring out various complementary aspects of the mystery of the Church. The Old Testament favours those images that are bound to the *people of God*. The New Testament offers images that are linked to Christ as the Head of this people which is his Body. Other images are drawn from pastoral life (sheepfold, flock, sheep),

753-757

from agriculture (field, olive grove, vineyard), from construction (dwelling place, stone, temple), and from family life (spouse, mother, family).

149. What is the origin and the fulfillment of the Church?

758-766 The Church finds her origin and fulfillment in the eternal plan of God.
778 She was prepared for in the Old Covenant with the election of Israel, the sign of the future gathering of all the nations. Founded by the words and actions of Jesus Christ, fulfilled by his redeeming death and Resurrection, the Church has been manifested as the mystery of salvation by the outpouring of the Holy Spirit at Pentecost. She will be perfected in the glory of heaven as the assembly of all the redeemed of the earth.

150. What is the mission of the Church?

767-769 The mission of the Church is to proclaim and establish the Kingdom of God begun by Jesus Christ among all peoples. The Church constitutes on earth the seed and beginning of this salvific Kingdom.

151. In what way is the Church a *mystery*?

770-773 The Church is a mystery in as much as in her visible reality there is
779 present and active a divine spiritual reality which can only be seen with the eyes of faith.

152. What does it mean to say that the Church is the universal sacrament of salvation?

774-776 This means that she is the sign and instrument both of the reconciliation
780 and communion of all of humanity with God and of the unity of the entire human race.

The Church: people of God, body of Christ, temple of the Spirit

153. Why is the Church the 'people of God'?

781 The Church is the 'people of God' because it pleased God to sanctify and
802-804 save men not in isolation but by making them into one people gathered together by the unity of the Father and the Son and the Holy Spirit.

154. What are the characteristics of the people of God?

782 One becomes a member of this people through faith in Christ and Baptism.
804 This people has for its *origin* God the Father; for its *head* Jesus Christ; for its *hallmark* the dignity and freedom of the sons of God; for its *law* the new commandment of love; for its *mission* to be the salt of the earth and the light of the world; and for its *destiny* the Kingdom of God, already begun on earth.

155. In what way does the people of God share in the three functions of Christ as Priest, Prophet and King?

The people of God participate in Christ's *priestly* office insofar as   783-786
the baptised are consecrated by the Holy Spirit to offer spiritual
sacrifices. They share in Christ's *prophetic* office when with a
supernatural sense of faith they adhere unfailingly to that faith and
deepen their understanding and witness to it. The people of God share
in his *kingly* office by means of service, imitating Jesus Christ who as
King of the universe made himself the servant of all, especially the poor
and the suffering.

156. In what way is the Church the body of Christ?

The risen Christ unites his faithful people to himself in an intimate   787-791
way by means of the Holy Spirit. In this way, those who believe in   805-806
Christ, in as much as they are close to him especially in the Eucharist,
are united among themselves in charity. They form one body, the
Church, whose unity is experienced in the diversity of its members and
its functions.

157. Who is the Head of this body?

Christ "is the Head of the body, the Church" (*Colossians* 1:18). The   792-795
Church lives from him, in him and for him. Christ and the Church make up 807
the "whole Christ" (Saint Augustine); "Head and members form, as it were,
one and the same mystical person" (Saint Thomas Aquinas).

158. Why is the Church called the "Bride of Christ"?

She is called the "Bride of Christ" because the Lord himself called   796
himself her "Spouse" (*Mark* 2:19). The Lord has loved the Church and   808
has joined her to himself in an everlasting covenant. He has given himself
up for her in order to purify her with his blood and "sanctify her"
(*Ephesians* 5:26), making her the fruitful mother of all the children of
God. While the term "body" expresses the unity of the "head" with the
members, the term "bride" emphasises the distinction of the two in their
personal relationship.

159. Why is the Church called the temple of the Holy Spirit?

She is so called because the Holy Spirit resides in the body which is the 797-798
Church, in her Head and in her members. He also builds up the Church in   809-810
charity by the Word of God, the sacraments, the virtues, and *charisms*.

> *"What the soul is to the human body, the Holy Spirit is to the members of Christ, that is, the body of Christ, which is the Church."* (Saint Augustine)

160. What are charisms?

799-801   Charisms are special gifts of the Holy Spirit which are bestowed on individuals for the good of others, the needs of the world, and in particular for the building up of the Church. The discernment of charisms is the responsibility of the Magisterium.

The Church is one, holy, catholic, and apostolic

161. Why is the Church *one*?

813-815   The Church is one because she has as her source and exemplar the unity
    866   of the Trinity of Persons in one God. As her Founder and Head, Jesus Christ re-established the unity of all people in one body. As her soul, the Holy Spirit unites all the faithful in communion with Christ. The Church has but one faith, one sacramental life, one apostolic succession, one common hope, and one and the same charity.

162. Where does the one Church of Christ subsist?

816   The one Church of Christ, as a society constituted and organised in the
870   world, subsists in (*subsistit in*) the Catholic Church, governed by the successor of Peter and the bishops in communion with him. Only through this Church can one obtain the fullness of the means of salvation since the Lord has entrusted all the blessings of the New Covenant to the apostolic college alone whose head is Peter.

163. How are non-Catholic Christians to be considered?

817-819   In the churches and ecclesial communities which are separated from
870   full communion with the Catholic Church, many elements of sanctification and truth can be found. All of these blessings come from Christ and lead to Catholic unity. Members of these churches and communities are incorporated into Christ by Baptism and so we recognise them as brothers.

164. How does one commit oneself to work for the unity of Christians?

820-822   The desire to restore the unity of all Christians is a gift from Christ and
866   a call of the Spirit. This desire involves the entire Church and it is pursued

by conversion of heart, prayer, fraternal knowledge of each other and theological dialogue.

165. In what way is the Church *holy*?

The Church is holy insofar as the Most Holy God is her author. Christ has given himself for her to sanctify her and make her a source of sanctification. The Holy Spirit gives her life with charity. In the Church one finds the fullness of the means of salvation. Holiness is the vocation of each of her members and the purpose of all her activities. The Church counts among her members the Virgin Mary and numerous Saints who are her models and intercessors. The holiness of the Church is the fountain of sanctification for her children who here on earth recognise themselves as sinners ever in need of conversion and purification.   823-829 867

166. Why is the Church called "*catholic*"?

The Church is *catholic*, that is *universal*, insofar as Christ is present in her: "Where there is Christ Jesus, there is the Catholic Church" (Saint Ignatius of Antioch). The Church proclaims the fullness and the totality of the faith; she bears and administers the fullness of the means of salvation; she is sent out by Christ on a mission to the whole of the human race.   830-831 868

167. Is the particular Church catholic?

Every *particular* Church (that is, a *diocese* or *eparchy*) is catholic. It is formed by a community of Christians who are in communion of faith and of the sacraments both with their bishop, who is ordained in apostolic succession, and with the Church of Rome which "presides in charity" (Saint Ignatius of Antioch).   832-835

168. Who belongs to the Catholic Church?

All human beings in various ways belong to or are ordered to the Catholic unity of the people of God. Fully incorporated into the Catholic Church are those who, possessing the Spirit of Christ, are joined to the Church by the bonds of the profession of faith, the sacraments, ecclesiastical government and communion. The baptised who do not enjoy full Catholic unity are in a certain, although imperfect, communion with the Catholic Church.   836-838

169. What is the relationship of the Catholic Church with the Jewish people?

The Catholic Church recognises a particular link with the Jewish people in the fact that God chose them before all others to receive his Word. To the   839-840

Jewish people belong "the sonship, the glory, the covenants, the giving of the law, the worship, the promises, and the patriarchs; and of their race, according to the flesh, is the Christ" (*Romans* 9:4,5). The Jewish faith, unlike other non-Christian religions, is already a response to the Revelation of God in the Old Covenant.

170. What is the bond that exists between the Catholic Church and non-Christian religions?

841-845   There is a bond between all peoples which comes especially from the common origin and end of the entire human race. The Catholic Church recognises that whatever is good or true in other religions comes from God and is a reflection of his truth. As such it can prepare for the acceptance of the Gospel and act as a stimulus towards the unity of humanity in the Church of Christ.

171. What is the meaning of the affirmation "Outside the Church there is no salvation"?

846-848   This means that all salvation comes from Christ, the Head, through the Church which is his body. Hence they cannot be saved who, knowing the Church as founded by Christ and necessary for salvation, would refuse to enter her or remain in her. At the same time, thanks to Christ and to his Church, those who through no fault of their own do not know the Gospel of Christ and his Church but sincerely seek God and, moved by grace, try to do his will as it is known through the dictates of conscience can attain eternal salvation.

172. Why must the Church proclaim the Gospel to the whole world?

849-851   The Church must do so because Christ has given the command: "Go therefore and make disciples of all nations, baptising them in the name of the Father and of the Son and of the Holy Spirit" (*Matthew* 28:19). This missionary mandate of the Lord has its origin in the eternal love of God who has sent his Son and the Holy Spirit because "he desires all men to be saved and to come to the knowledge of the truth" (1 *Timothy* 2:4).

173. In what sense is the Church missionary?

852-856   The Church, guided by the Holy Spirit, continues the mission of Christ himself in the course of history. Christians must, therefore, proclaim to everyone the Good News borne by Christ; and, following his path, they must be ready for self-sacrifice, even unto martyrdom.

174. Why is the Church *apostolic*?

857   The Church is apostolic in her *origin* because she has been built on "the
869   foundation of the Apostles" (*Ephesians* 2:20). She is apostolic in her

teaching which is the same as that of the Apostles. She is apostolic by reason of her *structure* insofar as she is taught, sanctified, and guided until Christ returns by the Apostles through their successors who are the bishops in communion with the successor of Peter.

175. In what does the mission of the Apostles consist?

The word "*Apostle*" means "one who is sent". Jesus, the One sent by the Father, called to himself twelve of his disciples and appointed them as his Apostles, making them the chosen witnesses of his Resurrection and the foundation of his Church. He gave them the command to continue his own mission saying, "As the Father has sent me, so I also send you" (*John* 20:21); and he promised to remain with them until the end of the world. 858-861

176. What is apostolic succession?

Apostolic succession is the transmission by means of the sacrament of Holy Orders of the mission and power of the Apostles to their successors, the bishops. Thanks to this transmission the Church remains in communion of faith and life with her origin, while through the centuries she carries on her apostolate for the spread of the Kingdom of Christ on earth. 861-865

The Faithful: hierarchy, laity, consecrated life

177. Who are the faithful?

The Christian faithful are those who, in as much as they have been incorporated in Christ through Baptism, have been constituted as the people of God; for this reason, since they have become sharers in Christ's priestly, prophetic and royal office in their own manner, they are called to exercise the mission which God has entrusted to the Church. There exists a true equality among them in their dignity as children of God. 871-872

178. How are the people of God formed?

Among the faithful by divine institution there exist *sacred ministers* who have received the sacrament of Holy Orders and who form the hierarchy of the Church. The other members of the Church are called the *laity*. In both the hierarchy and the laity there are certain of the faithful who are *consecrated* in a special manner to God by the profession of the evangelical counsels: chastity or celibacy, poverty, and obedience. 873
934

179. Why did Christ institute an ecclesiastical hierarchy?

Christ instituted an ecclesiastical hierarchy with the mission of feeding the people of God in his name and for this purpose gave it authority. The 874-876
935

hierarchy is formed of sacred ministers: bishops, priests, and deacons. Thanks to the sacrament of Orders, bishops and priests act in the exercise of their ministry in the name and person of Christ the Head. Deacons minister to the people of God in the *diakonia* (service) of word, liturgy, and charity.

180. How is the collegial dimension of Church ministry carried out?

877 After the example of the twelve Apostles who were chosen and sent out together by Christ, the unity of the Church's hierarchy is at the service of the communion of all the faithful. Every bishop exercises his ministry as a member of the episcopal college in communion with the Pope and shares with him in the care of the universal Church. Priests exercise their ministry in the presbyterate of the local Church in communion with their own bishop and under his direction.

181. Why does ecclesial ministry also have a personal character?

878-879 Ecclesial ministry also has a personal character in as much as each minister, in virtue of the sacrament of Holy Orders, is responsible before Christ who called him personally and conferred on him his mission.

182. What is the mission of the Pope?

880-882
936-937 The Pope, bishop of Rome and the successor of Saint Peter, is the perpetual, visible source and foundation of the unity of the Church. He is the vicar of Christ, the head of the college of bishops and pastor of the universal Church over which he has by divine institution full, supreme, immediate, and universal power.

183. What is the competence of the college of bishops?

883-885 The college of bishops in union with the Pope, and never without him, also exercises supreme and full authority over the Church.

184. How do the bishops carry out their mission of teaching?

888-890
939 Since they are authentic witnesses of the apostolic faith and are invested with the authority of Christ, the bishops in union with the Pope have the duty of proclaiming the Gospel faithfully and authoritatively to all. By means of a supernatural sense of faith, the people of God unfailingly adhere to the faith under the guidance of the living Magisterium of the Church.

185. When is the infallibility of the Magisterium exercised?

890-891 Infallibility is exercised when the Roman Pontiff, in virtue of his office as the Supreme Pastor of the Church, or the college of bishops, in union with the Pope especially when joined together in an Ecumenical

Council, proclaim by a definitive act a doctrine pertaining to faith or morals. Infallibility is also exercised when the Pope and bishops in their ordinary Magisterium are in agreement in proposing a doctrine as definitive. Every one of the faithful must adhere to such teaching with the obedience of faith.

186. How do bishops exercise their ministry of sanctification?

Bishops sanctify the Church by dispensing the grace of Christ by their ministry of the word and the sacraments, especially the Holy Eucharist, and also by their prayers, their example and their work.

893

187. How do the bishops exercise their function of governing?

Every bishop, insofar as he is a member of the college of bishops, bears collegially the care for all particular Churches and for the entire Church along with all the other bishops who are united to the Pope. A bishop to whom a particular Church has been entrusted governs that Church with the authority of his own sacred power which is ordinary and immediate and exercised in the name of Christ, the Good Shepherd, in communion with the entire Church and under the guidance of the successor of Peter.

894-896

188. What is the vocation of the lay faithful?

The lay faithful have as their own vocation to seek the Kingdom of God by illuminating and ordering temporal affairs according to the plan of God. They carry out in this way their call to holiness and to the apostolate, a call given to all the baptised.

897-900
940

189. How do the lay faithful participate in the priestly office of Christ?

They participate in it especially in the Eucharist by offering as a spiritual sacrifice "acceptable to God through Jesus Christ" (1 *Peter* 2:5) their own lives with all of their works, their prayers, their apostolic undertakings, their family life, their daily work and hardships borne with patience and even their consolations of spirit and body. In this way, even the laity, dedicated to Christ and consecrated by the Holy Spirit, offer to God the world itself.

901-903

190. How does the laity participate in the prophetic office?

They participate in it by welcoming evermore in faith the Word of Christ and proclaiming it to the world by the witness of their lives, their words, their evangelising action, and by catechesis. This evangelising action acquires a particular efficacy because it is accomplished in the ordinary circumstances of the world.

904-907
942

191. How do they participate in the kingly office?

908-913
943
The laity participate in the kingly function of Christ because they have received from him the power to overcome sin in themselves and in the world by self-denial and the holiness of their lives. They exercise various ministries at the service of the community and they imbue temporal activities and the institutions of society with moral values.

192. What is the consecrated life?

914-916
944
The consecrated life is a state of life recognised by the Church. It is a free response to a special call from Christ by which those consecrated give themselves completely to God and strive for the perfection of charity moved by the Holy Spirit. This consecration is characterised by the practice of the evangelical counsels.

193. What can the consecrated life give to the mission of the Church?

931-933
945
The consecrated life participates in the mission of the Church by means of a complete dedication to Christ and to one's brothers and sisters witnessing to the hope of the heavenly Kingdom.

I believe in the communion of saints

194. What is the meaning of the "communion of saints"?

946-953
960
This expression indicates first of all the common sharing of all the members of the Church in holy things (*sancta*): the faith, the sacraments, especially the Eucharist, the charisms, and the other spiritual gifts. At the root of this communion is love which "does not seek its own interests" (1 *Corinthians* 13:5) but leads the faithful to "hold everything in common" (*Acts* 4:32), even to put one's own material goods at the service of the most poor.

195. What else does "the communion of saints" mean?

954-959
961-962
This expression also refers to the communion between holy persons (*sancti*); that is, between those who by grace are united to the dead and risen Christ. Some are pilgrims on the earth; others, having passed from this life, are undergoing purification and are helped also by our prayers. Others already enjoy the glory of God and intercede for us. All of these together form in Christ one family, the Church, to the praise and glory of the Trinity.

Mary, Mother of Christ, Mother of the Church

196. In what sense is the Blessed Virgin Mary the Mother of the Church?

The Blessed Virgin Mary is the Mother of the Church in the order of grace because she gave birth to Jesus, the Son of God, the Head of the body which is the Church. When he was dying on the cross Jesus gave his mother to his disciple with the words, "Behold your mother" (*John* 19:27).

963-964
973

197. How does the Virgin Mary help the Church?

After the Ascension of her Son, the Virgin Mary aided the beginnings of the Church with her prayers. Even after her Assumption into heaven, she continues to intercede for her children, to be a model of faith and charity for all, and to exercise over them a salutary influence deriving from the superabundant merits of Christ. The faithful see in Mary an image and an anticipation of the resurrection that awaits them and they invoke her as advocate, helper, benefactress and mediatrix.

965-970
974-975

198. What kind of devotion is directed to the holy Virgin?

It is a singular kind of devotion which differs essentially from the cult of adoration given only to the Most Holy Trinity. This special veneration directed to Mary finds particular expression in the liturgical feasts dedicated to the Mother of God and in Marian prayers such as the holy Rosary which is a compendium of the whole Gospel.

971

199. In what way is the Blessed Virgin Mary the eschatological icon of the Church?

Looking upon Mary, who is completely holy and already glorified in body and soul, the Church contemplates in her what she herself is called to be on earth and what she will be in the homeland of heaven.

972
974-975

"I BELIEVE IN THE FORGIVENESS OF SINS"

200. How are sins remitted?

The first and chief sacrament for the forgiveness of sins is Baptism. For those sins committed after Baptism, Christ instituted the sacrament of Reconciliation or Penance through which a baptised person is reconciled with God and with the Church.

976-980
984-985

201. Why does the Church have the power to forgive sins?

981-983   The Church has the mission and the power to forgive sins because Christ
986-987   himself has conferred it upon her: "Receive the Holy Spirit, if you forgive
the sins of any, they are forgiven; if you retain the sins of any, they are
retained" (*John* 20:22-23).

"I BELIEVE IN THE RESURRECTION OF THE BODY"

202. What is the meaning of the term "body" (or "*flesh*") and what importance does it have?

990   The resurrection of the *flesh* is the literal formulation in the Apostles' Creed
1015   for the resurrection of the body. The term "flesh" refers to humanity in its state
of weakness and mortality. "The flesh is the hinge of salvation" (Tertullian).
We believe in God the Creator of the flesh; we believe in the Word made flesh
in order to redeem flesh; and we believe in the resurrection of flesh which is
the fulfillment of both the creation and the redemption of the flesh.

203. What is meant by the "resurrection of the body"?

990   This means that the definitive state of man will not be one in which his
spiritual soul is separated from his body. Even our mortal bodies will one
day come to life again.

204. What is the relationship between the Resurrection of Christ and our resurrection?

998   Just as Christ is truly risen from the dead and now lives forever, so he
1002-1003   himself will raise everyone on the last day with an incorruptible body:
"Those who have done good will rise to the resurrection of life and those
who have done evil to the resurrection of condemnation" (*John* 5:29).

205. What happens to our body and our soul after death?

992-1004   After death, which is the separation of the body and the soul, the
1016-1018   body becomes corrupt while the soul, which is immortal, goes to meet
the judgment of God and awaits its reunion with the body when it will
rise transformed at the time of the return of the Lord. *How* the
resurrection of the body will come about exceeds the possibilities of our
imagination and understanding.

206. What does it mean to die in Christ Jesus?

1005-1014   Dying in Christ Jesus means to die in the state of God's grace without any
1019   mortal sin. A believer in Christ, following his example, is thus able to transform

his own death into an act of obedience and love for the Father. "This saying is sure: if we have died with him, we will also live with him" (2 *Timothy* 2:11).

207. What is life everlasting?

Eternal life is that life which begins immediately after death. It will have no end. It will be preceded for each person by a particular judgment at the hands of Christ who is the Judge of the living and the dead. This particular judgment will be confirmed in the final judgment.

1020
1051

208. What is the particular judgment?

It is the judgment of immediate retribution which each one after death will receive from God in his immortal soul in accord with his faith and his works. This retribution consists in entrance into the happiness of heaven, immediately or after an appropriate purification, or entry into the eternal damnation of hell.

1021-1022
1051

209. What is meant by the term "heaven"?

By "heaven" is meant the state of supreme and definitive happiness. Those who die in the grace of God and have no need of further purification are gathered around Jesus and Mary, the angels and the saints. They thus form the Church of heaven, where they see God "face-to-face" (1 *Corinthians* 13:12). They live in a communion of love with the Most Blessed Trinity and they intercede for us.

1023-1026
1053

> *"True and subsistent life consists in this: the Father, through the Son and in the Holy Spirit, pouring out his heavenly gifts on all things without exception. Thanks to his mercy, we too, men that we are, have received the inalienable promise of eternal life."* (Saint Cyril of Jerusalem)

210. What is purgatory?

Purgatory is the state of those who die in God's friendship, assured of their eternal salvation, but who still have need of purification to enter into the happiness of heaven.

1030-1031
1054

211. How can we help the souls being purified in purgatory?

Because of the communion of saints, the faithful who are still pilgrims on earth are able to help the souls in purgatory by offering prayers in

1032

suffrage for them, especially the Eucharistic sacrifice. They also help them by almsgiving, indulgences, and works of penance.

212. In what does hell consist?

1033-1035   Hell consists in the eternal damnation of those who die in mortal sin
1056-1057   through their own free choice. The principal suffering of hell is eternal
separation from God in whom alone we can have the life and happiness for
which we were created and for which we long. Christ proclaimed this reality
with the words, "Depart from me, you cursed, into the eternal fire"
(*Matthew* 25:41).

213. How can one reconcile the existence of hell with the infinite goodness of God?

1036-1037   God, while desiring "all to come to repentance" (2 *Peter* 3:9),
nevertheless has created the human person to be free and responsible; and
he respects our decisions. Therefore, it is the human person who freely
excludes himself from communion with God if at the moment of death he
persists in mortal sin and refuses the merciful love of God.

214. In what does the final judgment consist?

1038-1041   The final or universal judgment consists in a sentence of happiness or
1058-1059   eternal condemnation, which the Lord Jesus will issue in regard to the "just
and the unjust" (*Acts* 24:15) when he returns as the Judge of the living and
the dead. After the last judgment, the resurrected body will share in the
retribution which the soul received at the particular judgment.

215. When will this judgment occur?

1040   This judgment will come at the end of the world and only God knows the
day and the hour.

216. What is the hope of the new heavens and the new earth?

1042-1050   After the final judgment the universe itself, freed from its bondage to
1060   decay, will share in the glory of Christ with the beginning of "the new
heavens" and a "new earth" (2 *Peter* 3:13). Thus, the fullness of the
Kingdom of God will come about, that is to say, the definitive realisation of
the salvific plan of God to "unite all things in Christ, things in heaven
and things on earth" (*Ephesians* 1:10). God will then be "all in all"
(1 *Corinthians* 15:28) in eternal life.

"Amen"

217. What is the meaning of the word *"Amen"* with which we conclude our profession of faith?

The Hebrew word *"Amen"*, which also concludes the last book of Sacred Scripture, some of the prayers of the New Testament, and the liturgical prayers of the Church, expresses our confident and total "yes" to what we professed in the Creed, entrusting ourselves completely to him who is the definitive *"Amen"* (*Revelation* 3:14), Christ the Lord.   1061-1065

In the painting displayed here, Jesus approaches his apostles at table and gives them Communion one by one. This is a genre of painting which evidences the great reverence of the Church for the Eucharist through the centuries.

"Without the Lord's day, we cannot live," the martyr Emeritus said at the beginning of the fourth century during one of the most savage persecutions of the Christians, that of Diocletian in 304 A.D. Accused of having participated in the Eucharist with his community, he admitted without reservation: "Without the Eucharist we cannot live." And one of the martyrs added: "Yes, I went to the gathering and I celebrated the Supper of the Lord with my brothers because I am a Christian" (*Acts of the Martyrs of Abitene*, chapter 11 and 7,16). For their fidelity to the Eucharist, the forty-nine North African martyrs were condemned to death. The Eucharistic Lord was the true life for Saturninus and his companion martyrs of Abitene in proconsular Africa. They preferred to die rather than be deprived of the Food of the Eucharist, the Bread of eternal life.

Saint Thomas Aquinas was accustomed at midday to enter the Church and place his forehead against the tabernacle with trust and surrender for an intimate and personal conversation with the Eucharistic Lord. This great theologian of the Middle Ages is also known for having composed the office for the feast of the Body of the Lord in which he set forth all his profound devotion for the Eucharist.

In the hymn for Morning Prayer (*Verbum supernum prodiens*), there is found a synthesis of the Catholic spirituality of the Eucharist:

"When he was about to be delivered over to death by the traitor and his accomplices, Jesus gave himself as the food of life to his disciples. To them he gave his Body and Blood under a twofold sign so that he could feed with a twofold substance the whole of man. By his birth he was given to us as a companion; by his seat at the table together with his chosen band, he was given to us as food; by his death he was given to us as our reward."

Aquinas, who called the Eucharist "the summit and perfection of all the spiritual life," could not but express the consciousness of the Church's faith for she believes in the Eucharist as the living presence of Jesus among us and as the indispensable nourishment for the spiritual life. The Eucharist is the golden thread that, beginning with the Last Supper, binds together all the ages of the Church's history up to ourselves today. The words of consecration, "This is my Body" and "This is my Blood" have been said at all times and places, even in the gulags, in the concentration camps, and in the thousands of prisons that are still here today. And it is upon this Eucharistic ground that the Church bases her life, her communion, and her mission.

———————

JOOS VAN WASSENHOVE, *Jesus Gives Communion to the Apostles*, National Gallery of the Marches, Urbino.

PART TWO

THE CELEBRATION
OF THE CHRISTIAN MYSTERY

SECTION ONE
THE SACRAMENTAL ECONOMY

The sacrifice of the cross is the fount of the sacramental economy of the Church. In this image Mary, who is a figure for the Church, gathers in her left hand the blood and water which flow from the open side of Christ and which are symbols of the Church's sacraments.

"But when they came to Jesus and saw that he was already dead, they did not break his legs; but one soldier thrust his lance into his side and immediately blood and water flowed out" (*John* 19:33-34).

Saint Augustine made this commentary:

"Christ our Lord, who in his suffering offered for us what in his being born he took from us, and who has become in eternity the greatest of priests, has commanded that this sacrifice which you see be offered, that is, his body and blood. Indeed, his body, rent by the lance, poured out water and blood by which he forgave our sins. Remembering this grace and working out your salvation (which is God then working in you), draw near and become a partaker of this altar with fear and trembling. See in this bread that very body which hung upon the cross and in this cup that very blood which gushed from his side. Even the ancient sacrifices of God's people prefigured in their manifold kinds this unique sacrifice that was to come. Christ is at the same time the lamb by reason of the innocence of his pure soul and the goat by reason of his flesh which was in the likeness of sinful flesh. Any other thing which in many and various ways might be prefigured in the sacrifices of the Old Testament points solely to this sacrifice which has been revealed in the New Testament.

Take then and eat the body of Christ since now you have become members of Christ in the body of Christ. Take and drink the blood of Christ. So as not to be cut off, eat that which unites you; so as not to think little of yourself, drink what is the price of your person. As this food, when you eat and drink of it, is transformed into yourself, so also do you transform yourselves into the body of Christ if you live in obedience and devotion to him. He indeed, when his passion was near, celebrated the Passover meal with his disciples. Taking the bread, he blessed it saying: *This is my body which will be given up for you.* In the same way, after having blessed it, he gave the cup saying: *This is my blood of the new covenant which will be shed for all for the forgiveness of sins.* This you have already read and heard of in the Gospel but you did not know that this Eucharist is the Son himself. Now with heart purified in an unstained conscience and with your body bathed in clean water, *look to him and you will be radiant with joy and your faces will not blush with shame*" (*Discourse*, 228B).

———

Chapel of the "Mother of the Redeemer," *Mosaic on the Wall of the Incarnation*, Vatican City.

218. What is the liturgy?

The liturgy is the celebration of the mystery of Christ and in particular his paschal mystery. Through the exercise of the priestly office of Jesus Christ the liturgy manifests in signs and brings about the sanctification of humankind. The public worship which is due to God is offered by the Mystical Body of Christ, that is, by its head and by its members. 1066-1070

219. What place does the liturgy occupy in the life of the Church?

The liturgy as the sacred action *par excellence* is the summit towards which the activity of the Church is directed and it is likewise the font from which all her power flows. Through the liturgy Christ continues the work of our redemption in, with and through his Church. 1071-1075

220. In what does the sacramental economy consist?

The sacramental economy consists in the communication of the fruits of Christ's redemption through the celebration of the sacraments of the Church, most especially that of the Eucharist, "until he comes" (1 *Corinthians* 11:26). 1076

CHAPTER ONE

THE PASCHAL MYSTERY IN THE AGE
OF THE CHURCH

THE LITURGY - WORK OF THE MOST HOLY TRINITY

221. In what way is the Father the source and the goal of the liturgy?

Through the liturgy the Father fills us with his blessings in the Word made flesh who died and rose for us and pours into our hearts the Holy Spirit. At the same time, the Church blesses the Father by her worship, praise and thanksgiving and begs him for the gift of his Son and the Holy Spirit. 1077-1083 1110

222. What is the work of Christ in the liturgy?

In the liturgy of the Church, it is his own paschal mystery that Christ signifies and makes present. By giving the Holy Spirit to his apostles he entrusted to them and their successors the power to make present the work of salvation through the Eucharistic sacrifice and the sacraments, in which he himself acts to communicate his grace to the faithful of all times and places throughout the world. 1084-1090

223. How does the Holy Spirit work in the liturgy of the Church?

1091-1109   The very closest cooperation is at work in the liturgy between the Holy
1112   Spirit and the Church. The Holy Spirit prepares the Church to encounter her
Lord. He recalls and manifests Christ to the faith of the assembly. He makes
the mystery of Christ really present. He unites the Church to the life and
mission of Christ and makes the gift of communion bear fruit in the Church.

THE PASCHAL MYSTERY IN THE SACRAMENTS
OF THE CHURCH

224. What are the sacraments and which are they?

1113-1131   The sacraments, instituted by Christ and entrusted to the Church, are
efficacious signs of grace perceptible to the senses. Through them divine life
is bestowed upon us. There are seven sacraments: Baptism, Confirmation,
Holy Eucharist, Penance, Anointing of the Sick, Holy Orders and
Matrimony.

225. What is the relationship of the sacraments to Christ?

1114-1116   The mysteries of Christ's life are the foundations of what he would
henceforth dispense in the sacraments, through the ministers of his Church.

> *"What was visible in our Saviour has passed over into his mysteries."*
> (Saint Leo the Great)

226. What is the link between the sacraments and the Church?

1117-1119   Christ has entrusted the sacraments to his Church. They are the
sacraments "of the Church" in a twofold sense: they are "from her" insofar
as they are actions of the Church which is the sacrament of Christ's action;
and they are "for her" in as much as they build up the Church.

227. What is the *sacramental* character?

1121   It is a spiritual "*seal*" bestowed by the sacraments of Baptism,
Confirmation, and Holy Orders. It is a promise and guarantee of divine
protection. By virtue of this seal the Christian is configured to Christ,
participates in a variety of ways in his priesthood and takes his part in the
Church according to different states and functions. He is, therefore, set apart
for divine worship and the service of the Church. Because this character is
indelible the sacraments that impress it on the soul are received only once
in life.

228. What is the relationship between the sacraments and faith?

The sacraments not only presuppose faith but with words and ritual elements they nourish, strengthen, and express it. By celebrating the sacraments, the Church professes the faith that comes from the apostles. This explains the origin of the ancient saying, "*lex orandi, lex credendi*," that is, the Church believes as she prays. 1122-1126 1133

229. Why are the sacraments efficacious?

The sacraments are efficacious *ex opere operato* ("by the very fact that the sacramental action is performed") because it is Christ who acts in the sacraments and communicates the grace they signify. The efficacy of the sacraments does not depend upon the personal holiness of the minister. However, the fruits of the sacraments do depend on the dispositions of the one who receives them. 1127-1128 1131

230. For what reason are the sacraments necessary for salvation?

For believers in Christ the sacraments, even if they are not all given to each of the faithful, are necessary for salvation because they confer sacramental grace, forgiveness of sins, adoption as children of God, conformation to Christ the Lord and membership in the Church. The Holy Spirit heals and transforms those who receive the sacraments. 1129

231. What is sacramental grace?

Sacramental grace is the grace of the Holy Spirit which is given by Christ and is proper to each sacrament. This grace helps the faithful in their journey towards holiness and so assists the Church as well to grow in charity and in her witness to the world. 1129, 1131 1134, 2003

232. What is the relationship between the sacraments and everlasting life?

In the sacraments the Church already receives a foretaste of eternal life, while "awaiting in blessed hope, the appearing in glory of our great God and saviour Christ Jesus" (*Titus* 2:13). 1130

CHAPTER TWO

THE SACRAMENTAL CELEBRATION
OF THE PASCHAL MYSTERY

CELEBRATING THE LITURGY OF THE CHURCH

Who celebrates?

233. Who acts in the liturgy?

1135-1137
1187
In the liturgy it is the *whole Christ* (*Christus Totus*) who acts, Head and Body. As our High Priest he celebrates with his body, which is the Church in heaven and on earth.

234. Who celebrates the heavenly liturgy?

1138-1139
The heavenly liturgy is celebrated by the angels, by the saints of the Old and New Testament, particularly the Mother of God, by the Apostles, by the martyrs, and by the "great multitude which no one could number from every nation, race, people, and tongue" (*Revelation* 7:9). When we celebrate the mystery of our salvation in the sacraments we participate in this eternal liturgy.

235. How does the Church on earth celebrate the liturgy?

1140-1144
1188
The Church on earth celebrates the liturgy as a priestly people in which each one acts according to his proper function in the unity of the Holy Spirit. The baptised offer themselves in a spiritual sacrifice; the ordained ministers celebrate according to the Order they received for the service of all the members of the Church; the bishops and priests act in the Person of Christ the Head.

How is the liturgy celebrated?

236. How is the liturgy celebrated?

1145
The celebration of the liturgy is interwoven with signs and symbols whose meaning is rooted in creation and in human culture. It is determined by the events of the Old Testament and is fully revealed in the Person and work of Christ.

237. From where do the sacramental signs come?

1146-1152
1189
Some come from created things (light, water, fire, bread, wine, oil); others come from social life (washing, anointing, breaking of bread). Still others come from the history of salvation in the Old Covenant (the Passover

rites, the sacrifices, the laying on of hands, the consecrations). These signs, some of which are normative and unchangeable, were taken up by Christ and are made the bearers of his saving and sanctifying action.

238. What is the link between the actions and the words in the celebration of the sacraments?

Actions and words are very closely linked in the celebration of the sacraments. Indeed, even if the symbolic actions are already in themselves a language, it is necessary that the words of the rite accompany and give life to these actions. The liturgical words and actions are inseparable both insofar as they are meaningful signs and insofar as they bring about what they signify. 1153-1155 1190

239. What are the criteria for the proper use of singing and music in liturgical celebrations?

Since song and music are closely connected with liturgical action they must respect the following criteria. They should conform to Catholic doctrine in their texts, drawn preferably from Sacred Scripture and liturgical sources. They should be a beautiful expression of prayer. The music should be of a high quality. Song and music should encourage the participation of the liturgical assembly. They should express the cultural richness of the people of God and the sacred and solemn character of the celebration. "He who sings, prays twice" (Saint Augustine). 1156-1158 1191

240. What is the purpose of holy images?

The image of Christ is the liturgical icon *par excellence*. Other images, representations of Our Lady and of the Saints, signify Christ who is glorified in them. They proclaim the same Gospel message that Sacred Scripture communicates by the word and they help to awaken and nourish the faith of believers. 1159-1161 1192

When is the liturgy celebrated?

241. What is the centre of the liturgical season?

The centre of the liturgical season is Sunday which is the foundation and kernel of the entire liturgical year and has its culmination in the annual celebration of Easter, the feast of feasts. 1163-1167 1193

242. What is the function of the liturgical year?

In the liturgical year the Church celebrates the whole mystery of Christ from his Incarnation to his return in glory. On set days the Church venerates 1168-1173 1194-1195 with special love the Blessed Virgin Mary, the Mother of God. The Church also keeps the memorials of saints who lived for Christ, who suffered with him, and who live with him in glory.

243. What is the Liturgy of the Hours?

1174-1178
1196
The Liturgy of the Hours, which is the public and common prayer of the Church, is the prayer of Christ with his body, the Church. Through the Liturgy of the Hours the mystery of Christ, which we celebrate in the Eucharist, sanctifies and transforms the whole of each day. It is composed mainly of psalms, other biblical texts, and readings from the Fathers and spiritual masters.

Where is the liturgy celebrated?

244. Does the Church need places in order to celebrate the liturgy?

1179-1181
1197-1198
The worship "in spirit and truth" (*John* 4:24) of the New Covenant is not tied exclusively to any place because Christ is the true temple of God. Through him Christians and the whole Church become temples of the living God by the action of the Holy Spirit. Nonetheless, the people of God in their earthly condition need places in which the community can gather to celebrate the liturgy.

245. What are sacred buildings?

1181
1198-1199
They are the houses of God, a symbol of the Church that lives in that place as well as of the heavenly Jerusalem. Above all they are places of prayer in which the Church celebrates the Eucharist and worships Christ who is truly present in the tabernacle.

246. What are the privileged places inside sacred buildings?

1182-1186
They are: the altar, the tabernacle, the place where the sacred Chrism and other holy oils are kept, the chair of the bishop (*cathedra*) or the chair of the priest, the ambo, the baptismal font, and the confessional.

LITURGICAL DIVERSITY AND THE UNITY OF THE MYSTERY

247. Why is the one Mystery of Christ celebrated by the Church according to various liturgical traditions?

1200-1204
1207-1209
The answer is that the unfathomable richness of the mystery of Christ cannot be exhausted by any single liturgical tradition. From the very beginning, therefore, this richness found expression among various peoples

and cultures in ways that are characterised by a wonderful diversity and complementarity.

248. What is the criterion that assures unity in the midst of plurality?

It is fidelity to the Apostolic Tradition, that is, the communion in the faith and in the sacraments received from the apostles, a communion that is both signified and guaranteed by apostolic succession. The Church is Catholic and therefore can integrate into her unity all the authentic riches of cultures. 1209

249. Is everything immutable in the liturgy?

In the liturgy, particularly in that of the sacraments, there are unchangeable elements because they are of divine institution. The Church is the faithful guardian of them. There are also, however, elements subject to change which the Church has the power and on occasion also the duty to adapt to the cultures of diverse peoples. 1205-1206

THE SEVEN SACRAMENTS OF THE CHURCH

The Seven Sacraments

Baptism
Confirmation
Holy Eucharist
Penance
Anointing of the Sick
Holy Orders
Matrimony

Septem Ecclesiæ Sacramenta

Baptísmum
Confirmátio
Eucharístia
Pænitæntia
Ùnctio infirmórum
Ordo
Matrimónium

The sacraments of the Church are the fruit of the redemptive sacrifice of Jesus on the cross. The triptych portrays a church in which the seven sacraments are celebrated. At the centre the cross is raised in a predominant way.

At the feet of the Crucified Christ, there is Mary, heartbroken, supported by John and the holy women. In the background a priest celebrating Mass elevates the Host after the consecration to show that the sacrifice of the cross is made present again in the Eucharistic celebration under the forms of bread and wine.

In the square to the left which shows a side chapel, the sacraments of Baptism, Confirmation, administered by the bishop, and Penance are portrayed. The one on the right depicts the sacraments of Holy Orders, again administered by the bishop, Matrimony, and Anointing of the Sick.

ROGIER VAN DER WEYDEN, *Triptych of the Seven Sacraments*, Koninklijk Museum of the Fine Arts, Antwerp.

250. How are the sacraments of the Church divided?

The sacraments are divided into: the sacraments of Christian initiation 1210-1211 (Baptism, Confirmation, and Holy Eucharist); the sacraments of healing (Penance and Anointing of the Sick); and the sacraments at the service of communion and mission (Holy Orders and Matrimony). The sacraments touch all the important moments of Christian life. All of the sacraments are ordered to the Holy Eucharist "as to their end" (Saint Thomas Aquinas).

CHAPTER ONE

THE SACRAMENTS OF CHRISTIAN INITIATION

251. How is Christian initiation brought about?

Christian initiation is accomplished by means of the sacraments which 1212 establish the *foundations* of Christian life. The faithful born anew by 1275 Baptism are strengthened by Confirmation and are then nourished by the Eucharist.

THE SACRAMENT OF BAPTISM

252. What names are given to the first sacrament of initiation?

This sacrament is primarily called *Baptism* because of the central rite 1213-1216 with which it is celebrated. To baptise means to "immerse" in water. The one 1276-1277 who is baptised is immersed into the death of Christ and rises with him as a "new creature" (2 *Corinthians* 5:17). This sacrament is also called the "bath of regeneration and renewal in the Holy Spirit" (*Titus* 3:5); and it is called "enlightenment" because the baptised becomes "a son of light" (*Ephesians* 5:8).

253. How is Baptism prefigured in the Old Covenant?

In the Old Covenant Baptism was prefigured in various ways: *water*, 1217-1222 seen as source of life and of death; in *the Ark of Noah*, which saved by means of water; in *the passing through the Red Sea*, which liberated Israel from Egyptian slavery; in *the crossing of the Jordan River*, that brought Israel into the promised land which is the image of eternal life.

254. Who brought to fulfillment those prefigurations?

All the Old Covenant prefigurations find their fulfillment in Jesus Christ. 1223-1224 At the beginning of his public life Jesus had himself baptised by John the Baptist in the Jordan. On the cross, blood and water, signs of Baptism and the Eucharist, flowed from his pierced side. After his Resurrection he gave to his apostles this mission: "Go forth and make disciples of all nations, baptising them in the name of the Father and of the Son and of the Holy Spirit" (*Matthew* 28:19).

255. Starting when and to whom has the Church administered Baptism?

1226-1228 From the day of Pentecost, the Church has administered Baptism to anyone who believes in Jesus Christ.

256. In what does the essential rite of Baptism consist?

1229-1245
1278 The essential rite of this sacrament consists in immersing the candidate in water or pouring water over his or her head while invoking the name of the Father and the Son and the Holy Spirit.

257. Who can receive Baptism?

1246-1252 Every person not yet baptised is able to receive Baptism.

258. Why does the Church baptise infants?

1250 The Church baptises infants because they are born with original sin. They need to be freed from the power of the Evil One and brought into that realm of freedom which belongs to the children of God.

259. What is required of one who is to be baptised?

1253-1255 Everyone who is to be baptised is required to make a profession of faith. This is done personally in the case of an adult or by the parents and by the Church in the case of infants. Also the godfather or the godmother and the whole ecclesial community share the responsibility for baptismal preparation (catechumenate) as well as for the development and safeguarding of the faith and grace given at Baptism.

260. Who can baptise?

1256
1284 The ordinary ministers of Baptism are the bishop and the priest. In the Latin Church the deacon also can baptise. In case of necessity any person can baptise provided he has the intention of doing what the Church does. This is done by pouring water on the head of the candidate while saying the Trinitarian formula for Baptism: "I baptise you in the name of the Father and of the Son and of the Holy Spirit".

261. Is Baptism necessary for salvation?

Baptism is necessary for salvation for all those to whom the Gospel has been proclaimed and who have had the possibility of asking for this sacrament.

1257

262. Is it possible to be saved without Baptism?

Since Christ died for the salvation of all, those can be saved without Baptism who die for the faith (*Baptism of blood*). Catechumens and all those who, even without knowing Christ and the Church, still (under the impulse of grace) sincerely seek God and strive to do his will can also be saved without Baptism (*Baptism of desire*). The Church in her liturgy entrusts children who die without Baptism to the mercy of God.

1258-1261
1281-1283

263. What are the effects of Baptism?

Baptism takes away original sin, all personal sins and all punishment due to sin. It makes the baptised person a participant in the divine life of the Trinity through sanctifying grace, the grace of justification which incorporates one into Christ and into his Church. It gives one a share in the priesthood of Christ and provides the basis for communion with all Christians. It bestows the theological virtues and the gifts of the Holy Spirit. A baptised person belongs forever to Christ. He is marked with the indelible seal of Christ (*character*).

1262-1274
1279-1280

264. What is the meaning of the Christian name received at Baptism?

The name is important because God knows each of us by name, that is, in our uniqueness as persons. In Baptism a Christian receives his or her own name in the Church. It should preferably be the name of a saint who might offer the baptised a model of sanctity and an assurance of his or her intercession before God.

2156-2159
2167

THE SACRAMENT OF CONFIRMATION

265. What place does Confirmation have in the divine plan of salvation?

In the Old Testament the prophets announced that the Spirit of the Lord would rest on the awaited Messiah and on the entire messianic people. The whole life and mission of Jesus were carried out in total communion with the Holy Spirit. The apostles received the Holy Spirit at Pentecost and proclaimed "the great works of God" (*Acts* 2:11). They gave the gift of the

1285-1288
1315

same Spirit to the newly baptised by the laying on of hands. Down through the centuries, the Church has continued to live by the Spirit and to impart him to her children.

266. Why is this sacrament called *Chrismation* or *Confirmation*?

1289   It is called *Chrismation* (in the Eastern Churches: Anointing with holy myron or chrism) because the essential rite of the sacrament is anointing with chrism. It is called *Confirmation* because it confirms and strengthens baptismal grace.

267. What is the essential rite of Confirmation?

1290-1301   The essential rite of Confirmation is the anointing with Sacred Chrism
1318   (oil mixed with balsam and consecrated by the bishop), which is done by the
1320-1321   laying on of the hand of the minister who pronounces the sacramental words proper to the rite. In the West this anointing is done on the forehead of the baptised with the words, "Be sealed with the gift of the Holy Spirit". In the Eastern Churches of the Byzantine rite this anointing is also done on other parts of the body with the words, "The seal of the gift of the Holy Spirit".

268. What is the effect of Confirmation?

1302-1305   The effect of Confirmation is a special outpouring of the Holy Spirit like
1316-1317   that of Pentecost. This outpouring impresses on the soul an indelible character and produces a growth in the grace of Baptism. It roots the recipient more deeply in divine sonship, binds him more firmly to Christ and to the Church and reinvigorates the gifts of the Holy Spirit in his soul. It gives a special strength to witness to the Christian faith.

269. Who can receive this sacrament?

1306-1311   Only those already baptised can and should receive this sacrament which
1319   can be received only once. To receive Confirmation efficaciously the candidate must be in the state of grace.

270. Who is the minister of Confirmation?

1312-1314   The original minister of Confirmation is the bishop. In this way the link between the confirmed and the Church in her apostolic dimension is made manifest. When a priest confers this sacrament, as ordinarily happens in the East and in special cases in the West, the link with the bishop and with the Church is expressed by the priest who is the collaborator of the bishop and by the Sacred Chrism, consecrated by the bishop himself.

THE SACRAMENT OF THE EUCHARIST

271. What is the Eucharist?

The Eucharist is the very sacrifice of the Body and Blood of the Lord Jesus which he instituted to perpetuate the sacrifice of the cross throughout the ages until his return in glory. Thus he entrusted to his Church this memorial of his death and Resurrection. It is a sign of unity, a bond of charity, a paschal banquet, in which Christ is consumed, the mind is filled with grace, and a pledge of future glory is given to us.

1322-1323
1409

272. When did Jesus Christ institute the Eucharist?

Jesus instituted the Eucharist on Holy Thursday, "the night on which he was betrayed" (1 *Corinthians* 11:23), as he celebrated the Last Supper with his apostles.

1323
1337-1340

273. How did he institute the Eucharist?

After he had gathered with his apostles in the Cenacle, Jesus took bread in his hands. He broke it and gave it to them saying, "Take this and eat it, all of you; this is my Body which will be given up for you". Then, he took the cup of wine in his hands and said, "Take this and drink of this, all of you. This is the cup of my Blood, the Blood of the new and everlasting covenant. It will be shed for you and for all so that sins may be forgiven. Do this in memory of me".

1337-1340
1365, 1406

274. What does the Eucharist represent in the life of the Church?

It is the source and summit of all Christian life. In the Eucharist, the sanctifying action of God in our regard and our worship of him reach their high point. It contains the whole spiritual good of the Church, Christ himself, our Pasch. Communion with divine life and the unity of the people of God are both expressed and effected by the Eucharist. Through the Eucharistic celebration we are united already with the liturgy of heaven and we have a foretaste of eternal life.

1324-1327
1407

275. What are the names for this sacrament?

The unfathomable richness of this sacrament is expressed in different names which evoke its various aspects. The most common names are: the Eucharist, Holy Mass, the Lord's Supper, the Breaking of the Bread, the Eucharistic Celebration, the Memorial of the passion, death and Resurrection of the Lord, the Holy Sacrifice, the Holy and Divine Liturgy, the Sacred Mysteries, the Most Holy Sacrament of the Altar, and Holy Communion.

1328-1332

276. Where does the Eucharist fit in the divine plan of salvation?

1333-1344   The Eucharist was foreshadowed in the Old Covenant above all in the annual Passover meal celebrated every year by the Jews with unleavened bread to commemorate their hasty, liberating departure from Egypt. Jesus foretold it in his teaching and he instituted it when he celebrated the Last Supper with his apostles in a Passover meal. The Church, faithful to the command of her Lord, "Do this in memory of me" (1 *Corinthians* 11:24), has always celebrated the Eucharist, especially on Sunday, the day of the Resurrection of Jesus.

277. How is the celebration of the Holy Eucharist carried out?

1345-1355   The Eucharist unfolds in two great parts which together form one, single
1408   act of worship. The Liturgy of the Word involves proclaiming and listening to the Word of God. The Liturgy of the Eucharist includes the presentation of the bread and wine, the prayer or the anaphora containing the words of consecration, and communion.

278. Who is the minister for the celebration of the Eucharist?

1348   The celebrant of the Eucharist is a validly ordained priest (bishop or
1411   priest) who acts in the Person of Christ the Head and in the name of the Church.

279. What are the essential and necessary elements for celebrating the Eucharist?

1412   The essential elements are wheat bread and grape wine.

280. In what way is the Eucharist a *memorial* of the sacrifice of Christ?

1362-1367   The Eucharist is a *memorial* in the sense that it makes present and actual the sacrifice which Christ offered to the Father on the cross, once and for all on behalf of mankind. The sacrificial character of the Holy Eucharist is manifested in the very words of institution, "This is my Body which is given for you" and "This cup is the New Covenant in my Blood that will be shed for you" (*Luke* 22:19-20). The sacrifice of the cross and the sacrifice of the Eucharist are *one and the same sacrifice*. The priest and the victim are the same; only the manner of offering is different: in a bloody manner on the cross, in an unbloody manner in the Eucharist.

281. In what way does the Church participate in the Eucharistic sacrifice?

In the Eucharist the sacrifice of Christ becomes also the sacrifice of the members of his Body. The lives of the faithful, their praise, their suffering, their prayers, their work, are united to those of Christ. In as much as it is a sacrifice, the Eucharist is likewise offered for all the faithful, living and dead, in reparation for the sins of all and to obtain spiritual and temporal benefits from God. The Church in heaven is also united to the offering of Christ. 1368-1372 1414

282. How is Christ present in the Eucharist?

Jesus Christ is present in the Eucharist in a unique and incomparable way. He is present in a true, real and substantial way, with his Body and his Blood, with his Soul and his Divinity. In the Eucharist, therefore, there is present in a sacramental way, that is, under the Eucharistic species of bread and wine, Christ whole and entire, God and Man. 1373-1375 1413

283. What is the meaning of *transubstantiation*?

Transubstantiation means the change of the whole substance of bread into the substance of the Body of Christ and of the whole substance of wine into the substance of his Blood. This change is brought about in the Eucharistic prayer through the efficacy of the Word of Christ and by the action of the Holy Spirit. However, the outward characteristics of bread and wine, that is the "Eucharistic species", remain unaltered. 1376-1377 1413

284. Does the breaking of the bread divide Christ?

The breaking of the bread does not divide Christ. He is present whole and entire in each of the Eucharistic species and in each of their parts. 1377

285. How long does the presence of Christ last in the Eucharist?

The presence of Christ continues in the Eucharist as long as the Eucharistic species subsist. 1377

286. What kind of worship is due to the sacrament of the Eucharist?

The worship due to the sacrament of the Eucharist, whether during the celebration of the Mass or outside it, is the worship of *latria*, that is, the adoration given to God alone. The Church guards with the greatest care Hosts that have been consecrated. She brings them to the sick and to other persons who find it impossible to participate at Mass. She also presents them for the solemn adoration of the faithful and she bears them in 1378-1381 1418 processions. The Church encourages the faithful to make frequent visits to adore the Blessed Sacrament reserved in the tabernacle.

287. Why is the Holy Eucharist the paschal banquet?

1382-1384   The Holy Eucharist is the paschal banquet in as much as Christ
1391-1396   sacramentally makes present his Passover and gives us his Body and Blood, offered as food and drink, uniting us to himself and to one another in his sacrifice.

288. What is the meaning of the altar?

1383   The *altar* is the symbol of Christ himself who is present both as
1410   sacrificial victim (the altar of the sacrifice) and as food from heaven which is given to us (the table of the Lord).

289. When does the Church oblige her members to participate at Holy Mass?

1389   The Church obliges the faithful to participate at Holy Mass every Sunday
1417   and on holy days of obligation. She recommends participation at Holy Mass on other days as well.

290. When must one receive Holy Communion?

1389   The Church recommends that the faithful, if they have the required dispositions, receive Holy Communion whenever they participate at Holy Mass. However, the Church obliges them to receive Holy Communion at least once a year during the Easter season.

291. What is required to receive Holy Communion?

1385-1389   To receive Holy Communion one must be fully incorporated into the
1415   Catholic Church and be in the state of grace, that is, not conscious of being in mortal sin. Anyone who is conscious of having committed a grave sin must first receive the sacrament of Reconciliation before going to Communion. Also important for those receiving Holy Communion are a spirit of recollection and prayer, observance of the fast prescribed by the Church, and an appropriate disposition of the body (gestures and dress) as a sign of respect for Christ.

292. What are the fruits of Holy Communion?

1391-1397   Holy Communion increases our union with Christ and with his Church. It
1416   preserves and renews the life of grace received at Baptism and Confirmation and makes us grow in love for our neighbour. It strengthens us in charity, wipes away venial sins and preserves us from mortal sin in the future.

293. When is it possible to give Holy Communion to other Christians?

Catholic ministers may give Holy Communion licitly to members of the 1398-1401 Oriental Churches which are not in full communion with the Catholic Church whenever they ask for it of their own will and possess the required dispositions. Catholic ministers may licitly give Holy Communion to members of other ecclesial communities only if, in grave necessity, they ask for it of their own will, possess the required dispositions, and give evidence of holding the Catholic faith regarding the sacrament.

294. Why is the Eucharist a "pledge of future glory"?

The Eucharist is a pledge of future glory because it fills us with every 1402-1405 grace and heavenly blessing. It fortifies us for our pilgrimage in this life and makes us long for eternal life. It unites us already to Christ seated at the right hand of the Father, to the Church in heaven and to the Blessed Virgin and all the saints.

In the Eucharist, we "break the one bread that provides the medicine of immortality, the antidote for death and the food that makes us live forever in Jesus Christ." (Saint Ignatius of Antioch)

CHAPTER TWO
THE SACRAMENTS OF HEALING

295. Why did Christ institute the sacraments of Penance and the Anointing of the Sick?

Christ, the physician of our soul and body, instituted these sacraments 1420-1421 because the new life that he gives us in the sacraments of Christian initiation 1426 can be weakened and even lost because of sin. Therefore, Christ willed that his Church should continue his work of healing and salvation by means of these two sacraments.

THE SACRAMENT OF PENANCE AND RECONCILIATION

296. What is the name of this sacrament?

It is called the sacrament of Penance, the sacrament of Reconciliation, 1422-1424 the sacrament of Forgiveness, the sacrament of Confession, and the sacrament of Conversion.

297. Why is there a sacrament of Reconciliation after Baptism?

1425-1426   Since the new life of grace received in Baptism does not abolish the
1484   weakness of human nature nor the inclination to sin (that is, *concupiscence*),
Christ instituted this sacrament for the conversion of the baptised who have
been separated from him by sin.

298. When did he institute this sacrament?

1485   The risen Lord instituted this sacrament on the evening of Easter when
he showed himself to his apostles and said to them, "Receive the Holy
Spirit. If you forgive the sins of any, they are forgiven; if you retain the sins
of any, they are retained" (*John* 20:22-23).

299. Do the baptised have need of conversion?

1427-1429   The call of Christ to conversion continues to resound in the lives of the
baptised. Conversion is a continuing obligation for the whole Church. She
is holy but includes sinners in her midst.

300. What is interior penance?

1430-1433   It is the movement of a "contrite heart" (*Psalm* 51:19) drawn by divine
1490   grace to respond to the merciful love of God. This entails sorrow for and
abhorrence of sins committed, a firm purpose not to sin again in the future
and trust in the help of God. It is nourished by hope in divine mercy.

301. What forms does penance take in the Christian life?

1434-1439   Penance can be expressed in many and various ways but above all in
fasting, prayer, and almsgiving. These and many other forms of penance can
be practiced in the daily life of a Christian, particularly during the time of
Lent and on the penitential day of Friday.

302. What are the essential elements of the sacrament of Reconciliation?

1440-1449   The essential elements are two: the acts of the penitent who comes to
repentance through the action of the Holy Spirit, and the absolution of the
priest who in the name of Christ grants forgiveness and determines the ways
of making satisfaction.

303. What are the acts of the penitent?

1450-1460   They are: a careful *examination of conscience*; *contrition* (or repentance),
1487-1492   which is perfect when it is motivated by love of God and imperfect if it rests
on other motives and which includes the determination not to sin again;

confession, which consists in the telling of one's sins to the priest; and *satisfaction* or the carrying out of certain acts of penance which the confessor imposes upon the penitent to repair the damage caused by sin.

304. Which sins must be confessed?

All grave sins not yet confessed, which a careful examination of conscience brings to mind, must be brought to the sacrament of Penance. The confession of serious sins is the only ordinary way to obtain forgiveness.

1456

305. When is a person obliged to confess mortal sins?

Each of the faithful who has reached the age of discretion is bound to confess his or her mortal sins at least once a year and always before receiving Holy Communion.

1457

306. Why can venial sins also be the object of sacramental confession?

The confession of venial sins is strongly recommended by the Church, even if this is not strictly necessary, because it helps us to form a correct conscience and to fight against evil tendencies. It allows us to be healed by Christ and to progress in the life of the Spirit.

1458

307. Who is the minister of this sacrament?

Christ has entrusted the ministry of Reconciliation to his apostles, to the bishops who are their successors and to the priests who are the collaborators of the bishops, all of whom become thereby instruments of the mercy and justice of God. They exercise their power of forgiving sins *in the name of the Father and of the Son and of the Holy Spirit*.

1461-1466
1495

308. To whom is the absolution of some sins reserved?

The absolution of certain particularly grave sins (like those punished by excommunication) is reserved to the Apostolic See or to the local bishop or to priests who are authorised by them. Any priest, however, can absolve a person who is in danger of death from any sin and excommunication.

1463

309. Is a confessor bound to secrecy?

Given the delicacy and greatness of this ministry and the respect due to people every confessor, without any exception and under very severe penalties, is bound to maintain "the sacramental seal" which means absolute secrecy about the sins revealed to him in confession.

1467

310. What are the effects of this sacrament?

1468-1470 The effects of the sacrament of Penance are: reconciliation with God and
1496 therefore the forgiveness of sins; reconciliation with the Church; recovery,
if it has been lost, of the state of grace; remission of the eternal punishment
merited by mortal sins, and remission, at least in part, of the temporal
punishment which is the consequence of sin; peace, serenity of conscience
and spiritual consolation; and an increase of spiritual strength for the
struggle of Christian living.

311. Can this sacrament be celebrated in some cases with a general confession and general absolution?

1480-1484 In cases of serious necessity (as in imminent danger of death) recourse
may be had to a communal celebration of Reconciliation with general
confession and general absolution, as long as the norms of the Church are
observed and there is the intention of individually confessing one's grave
sins in due time.

312. What are indulgences?

1471-1479 Indulgences are the remission before God of the temporal punishment
1498 due to sins whose guilt has already been forgiven. The faithful Christian
who is duly disposed gains the indulgence under prescribed conditions for
either himself or the departed. Indulgences are granted through the ministry
of the Church which, as the dispenser of the grace of redemption, distributes
the treasury of the merits of Christ and the Saints.

THE SACRAMENT OF ANOINTING OF THE SICK

313. How was sickness viewed in the Old Testament?

1499-1502 In the Old Testament sickness was experienced as a sign of weakness and
at the same time perceived as mysteriously bound up with sin. The prophets
intuited that sickness could also have a redemptive value for one's own sins
and those of others. Thus sickness was lived out in the presence of God from
whom people implored healing.

314. What is the significance of Jesus' compassion for the sick?

1503-1505 The compassion of Jesus towards the sick and his many healings of the
infirm were a clear sign that with him had come the Kingdom of God and
therefore victory over sin, over suffering, and over death. By his own
passion and death he gave new meaning to our suffering which, when united
with his own, can become a means of purification and of salvation for us and
for others.

315. What is the attitude of the Church towards the sick?

Having received from the Lord the charge to heal the sick, the Church strives to carry it out by taking care of the sick and accompanying them with her prayer of intercession. Above all, the Church possesses a sacrament specifically intended for the benefit of the sick. This sacrament was instituted by Christ and is attested by Saint James: "Is anyone among you sick? Let him call in the presbyters of the Church and let them pray over him and anoint him with oil in the name of the Lord" (*James* 5:14-15). 1506-1513 1526-1527

316. Who can receive the sacrament of Anointing of the Sick?

Any member of the faithful can receive this sacrament as soon as he or she begins to be in danger of death because of sickness or old age. The faithful who receive this sacrament can receive it several times if their illness becomes worse or another serious sickness afflicts them. The celebration of this sacrament should, if possible, be preceded by individual confession on the part of the sick person. 1514-1515 1528-1529

317. Who administers this sacrament?

This sacrament can be administered only by priests (bishops or presbyters). 1516, 1530

318. How is this sacrament celebrated?

The celebration of this sacrament consists essentially in an *anointing* with oil which may be blessed by the bishop. The anointing is on the forehead and on the hands of the sick person (in the Roman rite) or also on other parts of the body (in the other rites) accompanied by the *prayer* of the priest who asks for the special grace of this sacrament. 1517-1519 1531

319. What are the effects of this sacrament?

This sacrament confers a special grace which unites the sick person more intimately to the Passion of Christ for his good and for the good of all the Church. It gives comfort, peace, courage, and even the forgiveness of sins if the sick person is not able to make a confession. Sometimes, if it is the will of God, this sacrament even brings about the restoration of physical health. In any case this anointing prepares the sick person for the journey to the Father's House. 1520-1523 1532

320. What is Viaticum?

Viaticum is the Holy Eucharist received by those who are about to leave this earthly life and are preparing for the journey to eternal life. Communion in the body and blood of Christ who died and rose from the dead, received at the moment of passing from this world to the Father, is the seed of eternal life and the power of the Resurrection. 1524-1525

CHAPTER THREE

THE SACRAMENTS AT THE SERVICE
OF COMMUNION AND MISSION

321. What are the sacraments at the service of communion and mission?

1533-1535   Two sacraments, Holy Orders and Matrimony, confer a special grace for a particular mission in the Church to serve and build up the People of God. These sacraments contribute in a special way to ecclesial communion and to the salvation of others.

THE SACRAMENT OF HOLY ORDERS

322. What is the sacrament of Holy Orders?

1536   It is the sacrament through which the mission entrusted by Christ to his apostles continues to be exercised in the Church until the end of time.

323. Why is this sacrament called Holy Orders?

1537-1538   *Orders* designates an ecclesial body into which one enters by means of a special consecration (ordination). Through a special gift of the Holy Spirit, this sacrament enables the ordained to exercise a *sacred power* in the name and with the authority of Christ for the service of the People of God.

324. What place does the sacrament of Holy Orders have in the divine plan of salvation?

1539-1546   This sacrament was prefigured in the Old Covenant in the service of the
1590-1591   Levites, in the priesthood of Aaron, and in the institution of the seventy "Elders" (*Numbers* 11:25). These prefigurations find their fulfillment in Christ Jesus who by the sacrifice of the cross is the "one mediator between God and man" (1 *Timothy* 2:5), the "High Priest according to the order of Melchizedek" (*Hebrews* 5:10). The one priesthood of Christ is made present in the ministerial priesthood.

> *"Only Christ is the true priest, the others being only his ministers."*
> (Saint Thomas Aquinas)

325. What are the degrees that make up the sacrament of Holy Orders?

The sacrament of Holy Orders is composed of three degrees which are irreplaceable for the organic structure of the Church: the episcopate, the presbyterate and the diaconate.

1554
1593

326. What is the effect of episcopal ordination?

Episcopal ordination confers the fullness of the sacrament of Holy Orders. It makes the bishop a legitimate successor of the apostles and integrates him into the episcopal college to share with the Pope and the other bishops care for all the churches. It confers on him the offices of teaching, sanctifying, and ruling.

1557-1558
1594

327. What is the office confided to a bishop in a particular Church?

The bishop to whom the care of a particular Church is entrusted is the visible head and foundation of unity for that Church. For the sake of that Church, as vicar of Christ, he fulfills the office of shepherd and is assisted by his own priests and deacons.

1560-1561
1594

328. What is the effect of ordination to the priesthood?

The anointing of the Spirit seals the priest with an indelible, spiritual character that configures him to Christ the priest and enables him to act in the name of Christ the Head. As a co-worker of the order of bishops he is consecrated to preach the Gospel, to celebrate divine worship, especially the Eucharist from which his ministry draws its strength, and to be a shepherd of the faithful.

1562-1567
1595

329. How does a priest carry out his proper ministry?

A priest, although ordained for a universal mission, exercises his ministry in a particular Church. This ministry is pursued in sacramental brotherhood with other priests who form the "presbyterate". In communion with the bishop, and depending upon him, they bear responsibility for the particular Church.

1568

330. What is the effect of the ordination to the diaconate?

The deacon, configured to Christ the servant of all, is ordained for service to the Church. He carries out this service under the authority of his proper bishop by the ministry of the Word, of divine worship, of pastoral care and of charity.

1569-1571
1596

331. How is the sacrament of Holy Orders celebrated?

1572-1574   The sacrament of Holy Orders is conferred, in each of its three degrees,
1597   by means of the *imposition of hands* on the head of the ordinand by the
bishop who pronounces the solemn *prayer* of consecration. With this prayer
he asks God on behalf of the ordinand for the special outpouring of the Holy
Spirit and for the gifts of the Spirit proper to the ministry to which he is
being ordained.

332. Who can confer this sacrament?

1575-1576   Only validly ordained bishops, as successors of the apostles, can confer
1600   the sacrament of Holy Orders.

333. Who can receive this sacrament?

1577-1578   This sacrament can only be validly received by a baptised man. The
1598   Church recognises herself as bound by this choice made by the Lord
Himself. No one can demand to receive the sacrament of Holy Orders, but
must be judged suitable for the ministry by the authorities of the Church.

334. Is it necessary to be celibate to receive the sacrament of Holy Orders?

1579-1580   It is always necessary to be celibate for the episcopacy. For the
1599   priesthood in the Latin Church men who are practicing Catholics and
celibate are chosen, men who intend to continue to live a celibate life "for
the kingdom of heaven" (*Matthew* 19:12). In the Eastern Churches marriage
is not permitted after one has been ordained. Married men can be ordained
to the permanent diaconate.

335. What are the effects of the sacrament of Holy Orders?

1581-1589   This sacrament yields a special outpouring of the Holy Spirit which
configures the recipient to Christ in his triple office as Priest, Prophet, and
King, according to the respective degrees of the sacrament. Ordination
confers an indelible spiritual character and therefore cannot be repeated or
conferred for a limited time.

336. With what authority is the priestly ministry exercised?

1547-1553   Ordained priests in the exercise of their sacred ministry speak and act not
1592   on their own authority, nor even by mandate or delegation of the community,
but rather in the Person of Christ the Head and in the name of the Church.
Therefore, the ministerial priesthood differs essentially and not just in
degree from the priesthood common to all the faithful for whose service
Christ instituted it.

THE SACRAMENT OF MATRIMONY

337. What is the plan of God regarding man and woman?

God who is love and who created man and woman for love has called 1601-1605
them to love. By creating man and woman he called them to an intimate
communion of life and of love in marriage: "So that they are no longer two,
but one flesh" (*Matthew* 19:6). God said to them in blessing "Be fruitful and
multiply" (*Genesis* 1:28).

338. For what ends has God instituted Matrimony?

The marital union of man and woman, which is founded and endowed 1659-1660
with its own proper laws by the Creator, is by its very nature ordered to the
communion and good of the couple and to the generation and education of
children. According to the original divine plan this conjugal union is
indissoluble, as Jesus Christ affirmed: "What God has joined together, let no
man put asunder" (*Mark* 10:9).

339. How does sin threaten marriage?

Because of original sin, which caused a rupture in the God-given 1606-1608
communion between man and woman, the union of marriage is very often
threatened by discord and infidelity. However, God in his infinite mercy
gives to man and woman the grace to bring the union of their lives into
accord with the original divine plan.

340. What does the Old Testament teach about marriage?

God helped his people above all through the teaching of the Law and the 1609-1611
Prophets to deepen progressively their understanding of the unity and
indissolubility of marriage. The nuptial covenant of God with Israel
prepared for and prefigured the New Covenant established by Jesus Christ
the Son of God, with his spouse, the Church.

341. What new element did Christ give to Matrimony?

Christ not only restored the original order of Matrimony but raised it to 1612-1617
the dignity of a sacrament, giving spouses a special grace to live out their 1661
marriage as a symbol of Christ's love for his bride the Church: "Husbands,
love your wives as Christ loves the Church" (*Ephesians* 5:25).

342. Are all obliged to get married?

Matrimony is not an obligation for everyone, especially since God calls 1618-1620
some men and women to follow the Lord Jesus in a life of virginity or of
celibacy for the sake of the Kingdom of Heaven. These renounce the great

good of Matrimony to concentrate on the things of the Lord and seek to please him. They become a sign of the absolute supremacy of Christ's love and of the ardent expectation of his glorious return.

343. How is the sacrament of Matrimony celebrated?

1621-1624   Since Matrimony establishes spouses in a public state of life in the Church, its liturgical celebration is public, taking place in the presence of a priest (or of a witness authorised by the Church) and other witnesses.

344. What is matrimonial consent?

1625-1632   Matrimonial consent is given when a man and a woman manifest the will
1662-1663   to give themselves to each other irrevocably in order to live a covenant of faithful and fruitful love. Since consent constitutes Matrimony, it is indispensable and irreplaceable. For a valid marriage the consent must have as its object true Matrimony, and be a human act which is conscious and free and not determined by duress or coercion.

345. What is required when one of the spouses is not a Catholic?

1633-1637   A *mixed* marriage (between a Catholic and a baptised non-Catholic) needs for liceity the permission of ecclesiastical authority. In a case of *disparity of cult* (between a Catholic and a non-baptised person) a dispensation is required for validity. In both cases, it is essential that the spouses do not exclude the acceptance of the essential ends and properties of marriage. It is also necessary for the Catholic party to accept the obligation, of which the non-Catholic party has been advised, to persevere in the faith and to assure the baptism and Catholic education of their children.

346. What are the effects of the sacrament of Matrimony?

1638-1642   The sacrament of Matrimony establishes a perpetual and exclusive *bond* between the spouses. God himself seals the consent of the spouses. Therefore, a marriage which is ratified and consummated between baptised persons can never be dissolved. Furthermore, this sacrament bestows upon the spouses the grace necessary to attain holiness in their married life and to accept responsibly the gift of children and provide for their education.

347. What sins are gravely opposed to the sacrament of Matrimony?

1645-1648   Adultery and polygamy are opposed to the sacrament of Matrimony because they contradict the equal dignity of man and woman and the unity and exclusivity of married love. Other sins include the deliberate refusal of one's procreative potential which deprives conjugal love of the gift of children and divorce which goes against the indissolubility of marriage.

348. When does the Church allow the physical separation of spouses?

The Church permits the physical separation of spouses when for serious reasons their living together becomes practically impossible, even though there may be hope for their reconciliation. As long as one's spouse lives, however, one is not free to contract a new union, except if the marriage be null and be declared so by ecclesiastical authority.

1629
1649

349. What is the attitude of the Church towards those people who are divorced and then remarried?

The Church, since she is faithful to her Lord, cannot recognise the union of people who are civilly divorced and remarried. "Whoever divorces his wife and marries another, commits adultery against her; and if she divorces her husband and marries another, she commits adultery" (*Mark* 10:11-12). The Church manifests an attentive solicitude towards such people and encourages them to a life of faith, prayer, works of charity and the Christian education of their children. However, they cannot receive sacramental absolution, take Holy Communion, or exercise certain ecclesial responsibilities as long as their situation, which objectively contravenes God's law, persists.

1650-1651
1665

350. Why is the Christian family called a *domestic church*?

The Christian family is called the domestic church because the family manifests and lives out the communal and familial nature of the Church as the family of God. Each family member, in accord with their own role, exercises the baptismal priesthood and contributes towards making the family a community of grace and of prayer, a school of human and Christian virtue and the place where the faith is first proclaimed to children.

1655-1658
1666

CHAPTER FOUR

OTHER LITURGICAL CELEBRATIONS

THE SACRAMENTALS

351. What are the sacramentals?

These are sacred signs instituted by the Church to sanctify different circumstances of life. They include a prayer accompanied by the sign of the cross and other signs. Among the sacramentals which occupy an important place are: blessings, which are the praise of God and a prayer to obtain his gifts, the consecration of persons and the dedication of things for the worship of God.

1667-1672
1677-1678

352. What is an exorcism?

1673   When the Church asks with its authority in the name of Jesus that a person or object be protected against the power of the Evil One and withdrawn from his dominion, it is called an exorcism. This is done in ordinary form in the rite of Baptism. A solemn exorcism, called a *major exorcism*, can be performed only by a priest authorised by the bishop.

353. What forms of popular piety accompany the sacramental life of the Church?

1674-1676   The religious sense of the Christian people has always found expression
1679   in the various forms of piety which accompany the sacramental life of the Church such as the veneration of relics, visits to sanctuaries, pilgrimages, processions, the stations of the cross and the rosary. The Church sheds the light of faith upon and fosters authentic forms of popular piety.

CHRISTIAN FUNERALS

354. What is the relationship between the sacraments and the death of a Christian?

1680-1683   The Christian who dies in Christ reaches at the end of his earthly existence the fulfillment of that new life which was begun in Baptism, strengthened in Confirmation, and nourished in the Eucharist, the foretaste of the heavenly banquet. The meaning of the death of a Christian becomes clear in the light of the death and Resurrection of Christ our only hope. The Christian who dies in Christ Jesus goes "away from the body to be at home with the Lord" (2 *Corinthians* 5:8).

355. What do funeral rites express?

1684-1685   Although celebrated in different rites in keeping with the situations and traditions of various regions, funerals express the paschal character of Christian death in hope of the Resurrection. They also manifest the meaning of communion with the departed particularly through prayer for the purification of their souls.

356. What are the main moments in funerals?

1686-1690   Usually, funeral rites consist of four principal parts: welcoming the body of the deceased by the community with words of comfort and hope, the liturgy of the Word, the Eucharistic Sacrifice, and the farewell in which the soul of the departed is entrusted to God, the Source of eternal life, while the body is buried in the hope of the Resurrection.

This illustration portrays the Last Supper with the institution of the Eucharist in a grand, carpeted hall off the ground floor (cf. *Mark* 14:15).

"While they were eating, Jesus took bread, said the blessing, broke it, and giving it to his disciples said, 'Take and eat; this is my body.' Then he took a cup, gave thanks, and gave it to them, saying, 'Drink from it, all of you, for this is my blood of the covenant which will be shed on behalf of the many for the forgiveness of sins'" (*Matthew* 26:26-28).

In this image, Jesus is seated with the apostles around a table in the form of a chalice. On the table are the Eucharistic species: bread and wine. The hall which is displayed against a very elaborate architectural backdrop with buildings and a circular tabernacle with seven columns symbolises the Church which is the abode of the Eucharistic Christ. A significant detail is offered by the apostle John who rests his head upon Jesus' chest (cf. *John* 13:25). He displays the communion of love which the Eucharist produces in the faithful. It is the response of the disciple to the invitation of the Master:

"I am the vine; you are the branches. Whoever remains in me and I in him will bear much fruit... Remain in my love. If you keep my commandments, you will remain in my love" (*John* 15:5, 9-10).

The Eucharist is communion with Jesus and spiritual food to support the faithful in his daily struggle to keep the commandments:

"The Saviour...is always and wholly present to those who live in him. He provides for their every need. He is everything for them and does not allow them to turn their glance to any other thing or to seek any thing apart from him. Indeed there is nothing the saints need but him: he gives them life and growth; he nourishes them; he is their light and breath; he moulds in them the image of himself; he shines with the light of himself upon it and then offers himself to their sight. He is at once the nourishment and the One who nourishes. It is he who offers the bread of life and that which he offers is himself, the life of the living, fragrance to the one who breathes, the garment to the one who would put it on. Again it is he who enables us to walk and he is the way and also the place of rest, the end. We are his members; he is the head: is there need to do battle? He fights along with us and it is he who assigns victory to whom the honour is given. Do we win? Behold, he is the crown. Thus from every direction he leads our mind back to him and he does not allow us to turn to anything else nor be captivated by love of something else... From what we have said it should be clear that life in Christ does not concern the future only; rather it is already present for the saints who live and act in it" (N. Cabasilas, *Life in Christ*, 1, 13-15).

JACOB COPISTA, Illustration from the *Tetraevangelo*, Library of the Mechitarist Fathers, Vienna.

PART THREE

LIFE IN CHRIST

SECTION ONE
MAN'S VOCATION: LIFE IN THE SPIRIT

Mary, the *Panhagia* (*all holy*) is the masterpiece of the Holy Spirit (*Panhagion*). Her existence, from her immaculate conception to her glorious assumption into heaven, is completely sustained by the love of God. The Spirit of the Love of the Father and the Son makes of Mary a new creature, the new Eve. Her heart and mind are intent upon the adoration of and obedience to the heavenly Father. She is his beloved daughter and she is also dedicated to the acceptance and service of the Son whose mother and disciple she is. Her soul is likewise intent upon her surrender to and cooperation with the Holy Spirit for whom she is a treasured sanctuary.

In this image Mary is surrounded by angels playing musical instruments and making merry, her head crowned with the divine love of the Holy Spirit, symbolised by the dove. Mary is the mother and protector of the Church (at her feet there is a faint glimpse of a sacred edifice). Through her efficacious, motherly intercession with Jesus, she pours out upon the Church the abundance of heavenly graces (symbolised by the tuft of blooming roses).

Below, to the left, the apostle John in contemplation of Immaculate Mary represents every one of the faithful who sees in the Blessed Virgin the perfect model and likewise the teacher and guide for living in the Spirit.

The Cistercian abbot Christian (12th century) reflected upon how the apostles shared with Mary their spiritual experiences. Comparing them to the twelve stars which crown the Blessed Virgin, he wrote:

"Frequently they gathered around the most prudent Virgin like disciples around their teacher to learn more fully the truth about what she had done, the truth that they would preach to others at the right moment. Since she was divinely set apart and taught, she showed herself to be a true storehouse of heavenly wisdom since in her daily life she had been close as a singular companion to wisdom itself, namely her Son, and had taken to heart and faithfully kept the things she had seen and heard (*Sermon I on the Assumption of Blessed Mary*).

EL GRECO, *Saint John Contemplates the Immaculate Conception*, Museum of Santa Cruz, Toledo.

357. How is the Christian moral life bound up with faith and the sacraments?

What the symbol of faith professes, the sacraments communicate. 1691-1698
Indeed, through them the faithful receive the grace of Christ and the gifts of
the Holy Spirit which give them the capability of living a new life as
children of God in Christ whom they have received in faith.

"O Christian, recognise your dignity." (Saint Leo the Great)

CHAPTER ONE
THE DIGNITY OF THE HUMAN PERSON

MAN THE IMAGE OF GOD

358. What is the root of human dignity?

The dignity of the human person is rooted in his or her creation in the 1699-1715
image and likeness of God. Endowed with a spiritual and immortal soul,
intelligence and free will, the human person is ordered to God and called in
soul and in body to eternal beatitude.

OUR VOCATION TO BEATITUDE

359. How do we attain beatitude?

We attain beatitude by virtue of the grace of Christ which makes us 1716
participants in the divine life. Christ in the Gospel points out to his followers
the way that leads to eternal happiness: the beatitudes. The grace of Christ
also is operative in every person who, following a correct conscience, seeks
and loves the true and the good and avoids evil.

360. Why are the beatitudes important for us?

The beatitudes are at the heart of Jesus' preaching and they take up and 1716-1717
fulfill the promises that God made starting with Abraham. They depict the 1725-1726
very countenance of Jesus and they characterise authentic Christian life.
They reveal the ultimate goal of human activity, which is eternal happiness.

361. What is the relationship between the beatitudes and our desire for happiness?

The beatitudes respond to the innate desire for happiness that God has 1718-1719
placed in the human heart in order to draw us to himself. God alone can
satisfy this desire.

362. What is eternal happiness?

1720-1724   It is the vision of God in eternal life in which we are fully "partakers of
1727-1729   the divine nature" (2 *Peter* 1:4), of the glory of Christ and of the joy of the
trinitarian life. This happiness surpasses human capabilities. It is a
supernatural and gratuitous gift of God just as is the grace which leads to it.
This promised happiness confronts us with decisive moral choices
concerning earthly goods and urges us to love God above all things.

MAN'S FREEDOM

363. What is freedom?

1730-1733   Freedom is the power given by God to act or not to act, to do this or to
1743-1744   do that, and so to perform deliberate actions on one's own responsibility.
Freedom characterises properly human acts. The more one does what is
good, the freer one becomes. Freedom attains its proper perfection when it
is directed towards God, the highest good and our beatitude. Freedom
implies also the possibility of choosing between good and evil. The choice
of evil is an abuse of freedom and leads to the slavery of sin.

364. What is the relationship between freedom and responsibility?

1734-1737   Freedom makes people responsible for their actions to the extent that
1745-1746   they are voluntary, even if the imputability and responsibility for an action
can be diminished or sometimes cancelled by ignorance, inadvertence,
duress, fear, inordinate attachments, or habit.

365. Why does everyone have a right to exercise freedom?

1738   The right to the exercise of freedom belongs to everyone because it is
1747   inseparable from his or her dignity as a human person. Therefore this right
must always be respected, especially in moral and religious matters, and it
must be recognised and protected by civil authority within the limits of the
common good and a just public order.

366. What place does human freedom have in the plan of salvation?

1739-1742   Our freedom is weakened because of original sin. This weakness is
1748   intensified because of successive sins. Christ, however, set us free "so that
we should remain free" (*Galatians* 5:1). With his grace, the Holy Spirit
leads us to spiritual freedom to make us free co-workers with him in the
Church and in the world.

367. What are the sources of the morality of human acts?

The morality of human acts depends on three sources: *the object chosen*, 1749-1754
either a true or apparent good; *the intention* of the subject who acts, that is, 1757-1758
the purpose for which the subject performs the act; and *the circumstances* of
the act, which include its consequences.

368. When is an act morally good?

An act is morally good when it assumes simultaneously the goodness of 1755-1756
the object, of the end, and of the circumstances. A chosen object can by 1759-1760
itself vitiate an act in its entirety, even if the intention is good. It is not licit
to do evil so that good may result from it. An evil end corrupts the action,
even if the object is good in itself. On the other hand, a good end does not
make an act good if the object of that act is evil, since the end does not
justify the means. Circumstances can increase or diminish the responsibility
of the one who is acting but they cannot change the moral quality of the acts
themselves. They never make good an act which is in itself evil.

369. Are there acts which are always illicit?

There are some acts which, in and of themselves, are always illicit by 1756, 1761
reason of their object (for example, blasphemy, homicide, adultery).
Choosing such acts entails a disorder of the will, that is, a moral evil which
can never be justified by appealing to the good effects which could possibly
result from them.

THE MORALITY OF THE PASSIONS

370. What are the passions?

The passions are the feelings, the emotions or the movements of the 1762-1766
sensible appetite - natural components of human psychology - which incline 1771-1772
a person to act or not to act in view of what is perceived as good or evil. The
principal passions are love and hatred, desire and fear, joy, sadness, and
anger. The chief passion is love which is drawn by the attraction of the good.
One can only love what is good, real or apparent.

371. Are the passions morally good or bad?

The passions insofar as they are movements of the sensible appetite are 1767-1770
neither good nor bad in themselves. They are good when they contribute to 1773-1775
a good action and they are evil in the opposite case. They can be taken up
into the virtues or perverted by the vices.

The Moral Conscience

372. What is the moral conscience?

1776-1780   Moral conscience, present in the heart of the person, is a judgment of
1795-1797   reason which at the appropriate moment enjoins him to do good and to avoid
evil. Thanks to moral conscience, the human person perceives the moral
quality of an act to be done or which has already been done, permitting him
to assume responsibility for the act. When attentive to moral conscience, the
prudent person can hear the voice of God who speaks to him or her.

373. What does the dignity of the human person imply for the moral conscience?

1780-1782   The dignity of a human person requires the uprightness of a moral
1798   conscience (which is to say that it be in accord with what is just and good
according to reason and the law of God). Because of this personal dignity,
no one may be forced to act contrary to conscience; nor, within the limits of
the common good, be prevented from acting according to it, especially in
religious matters.

374. How is a moral conscience formed to be upright and truthful?

1783-1788   An upright and true moral conscience is formed by education and by
1799-1800   assimilating the Word of God and the teaching of the Church. It is supported
by the gifts of the Holy Spirit and helped by the advice of wise people.
Prayer and an examination of conscience can also greatly assist one's moral
formation.

375. What norms must conscience always follow?

1789   There are three general norms: 1) one may never do evil so that good may
result from it; 2) the so-called *Golden Rule*, "Whatever you wish that men
would do to you, do so to them" (*Matthew* 7:12); 3) charity always proceeds
by way of respect for one's neighbour and his conscience, even though this
does not mean accepting as good something that is objectively evil.

376. Can a moral conscience make erroneous judgments?

1790-1794   A person must always obey the certain judgment of his own conscience
1801-1802   but he could make erroneous judgments for reasons that may not always
exempt him from personal guilt. However, an evil act committed through
involuntary ignorance is not imputable to the person, even though the act
remains objectively evil. One must therefore work to correct the errors of
moral conscience.

THE VIRTUES

377. What is a virtue?

A virtue is an habitual and firm disposition to do the good. "The goal of a virtuous life is to become like God" (Saint Gregory of Nyssa). There are human virtues and theological virtues. 1803, 1833

378. What are the human virtues?

The human virtues are habitual and stable perfections of the intellect and will that govern our actions, order our passions and guide our conduct according to reason and faith. They are acquired and strengthened by the repetition of morally good acts and they are purified and elevated by divine grace. 1804 1810-1811 1834, 1839

379. What are the principal human virtues?

The principal human virtues are called the *cardinal* virtues, under which all the other virtues are grouped and which are the hinges of a virtuous life. The cardinal virtues are: prudence, justice, fortitude, and temperance. 1805 1834

380. What is prudence?

Prudence disposes reason to discern in every circumstance our true good and to choose the right means for achieving it. Prudence guides the other virtues by pointing out their rule and measure. 1806 1835

381. What is justice?

Justice consists in the firm and constant will to give to others their due. Justice towards God is called "the virtue of religion." 1807 1836

382. What is fortitude?

Fortitude assures firmness in difficulties and constancy in the pursuit of the good. It reaches even to the ability of possibly sacrificing one's own life for a just cause. 1808 1837

383. What is temperance?

Temperance moderates the attraction of pleasures, assures the mastery of the will over instincts and provides balance in the use of created goods. 1809 1838

384. What are the theological virtues?

The theological virtues have God himself as their origin, motive and direct object. Infused with sanctifying grace, they bestow on one the capacity to live in a relationship with the Trinity. They are the foundation 1812-1813 1840-1841

and the energising force of the Christian's moral activity and they give life
to the human virtues. They are the pledge of the presence and action of the
Holy Spirit in the faculties of the human being.

385. What are the theological virtues?

1813   The theological virtues are faith, hope, and charity.

386. What is the virtue of faith?

1814-1816   Faith is the theological virtue by which we believe in God and all that he
1842   has revealed to us and that the Church proposes for our belief because God
is Truth itself. By faith the human person freely commits himself to God.
Therefore, the believer seeks to know and do the will of God because "faith
works through charity" (*Galatians* 5:6).

387. What is hope?

1817-1821   Hope is the theological virtue by which we desire and await from God
1843   eternal life as our happiness, placing our trust in Christ's promises and
relying on the help of the grace of the Holy Spirit to merit it and to persevere
to the end of our earthly life.

388. What is charity?

1822-1829   Charity is the theological virtue by which we love God above all things
1844   and our neighbour as ourselves for the love of God. Jesus makes charity the
new commandment, the fullness of the law. "It is the bond of perfection"
(*Colossians* 3:14) and the foundation of the other virtues to which it gives
life, inspiration, and order. Without charity "I am nothing" and "I gain
nothing" (1 *Corinthians* 13:1-3).

389. What are the gifts of the Holy Spirit?

1830-1831   The gifts of the Holy Spirit are permanent dispositions which make us
1845   docile in following divine inspirations. They are seven: wisdom,
understanding, counsel, fortitude, knowledge, piety, and fear of the Lord.

390. What are the fruits of the Holy Spirit?

1832   The *fruits* of the Holy Spirit are perfections formed in us as the first fruits
of eternal glory. The tradition of the Church lists twelve of them: charity, joy,
peace, patience, kindness, goodness, generosity, gentleness, faithfulness,
modesty, self-control, and chastity (*Galatians* 5:22-23, Vulgate).

Sin

391. What does the acceptance of God's mercy require from us?

It requires that we admit our faults and repent of our sins. God himself by his Word and his Spirit lays bare our sins and gives us the truth of conscience and the hope of forgiveness. 1846-1848 1870

392. What is sin?

Sin is "a word, an act, or a desire contrary to the eternal Law" (Saint Augustine). It is an offense against God in disobedience to his love. It wounds human nature and injures human solidarity. Christ in his passion fully revealed the seriousness of sin and overcame it with his mercy. 1849-1851 1871-1872

393. Is there a variety of sins?

There are a great many kinds of sins. They can be distinguished according to their object or according to the virtues or commandments which they violate. They can directly concern God, neighbour, or ourselves. They can also be divided into sins of thought, of word, of deed, or of omission. 1852-1853 1873

394. How are sins distinguished according to their gravity?

A distinction is made between mortal and venial sin. 1854

395. When does one commit a mortal sin?

One commits a mortal sin when there are simultaneously present: grave matter, full knowledge, and deliberate consent. This sin destroys charity in us, deprives us of sanctifying grace, and, if unrepented, leads us to the eternal death of hell. It can be forgiven in the ordinary way by means of the sacraments of Baptism and of Penance or Reconciliation. 1855-1861 1874

396. When does one commit a venial sin?

One commits a venial sin, which is essentially different from a mortal sin, when the matter involved is less serious or, even if it is grave, when full knowledge or complete consent are absent. Venial sin does not break the covenant with God but it weakens charity and manifests a disordered affection for created goods. It impedes the progress of a soul in the exercise of the virtues and in the practice of moral good. It merits temporal punishment which purifies. 1862-1864 1875

397. How does sin proliferate?

1865, 1876   Sin creates a proclivity to sin; it engenders vice by repetition of the same acts.

398. What are vices?

1866-1867   Vices are the opposite of virtues. They are perverse habits which darken the conscience and incline one to evil. The vices can be linked to the seven, so-called, *capital* sins which are: pride, avarice, envy, anger, lust, gluttony, and sloth or acedia.

399. Do we have any responsibility for sins committed by others?

1868   We do have such a responsibility when we culpably cooperate with them.

400. What are *structures* of sin?

1869   *Structures* of sin are social situations or institutions that are contrary to the divine law. They are the expression and effect of personal sins.

CHAPTER TWO

THE HUMAN COMMUNITY

THE PERSON AND SOCIETY

401. In what does the social dimension of man consist?

1877-1880   Together with the personal call to beatitude, the human person has a
1890-1891   communal dimension as an essential component of his nature and vocation. Indeed, all are called to the same end, God himself. There is a certain resemblance between the communion of the divine Persons and the fraternity that people are to establish among themselves in truth and love. Love of neighbour is inseparable from love for God.

402. What is the relationship between the person and society?

1881-1882   The human *person* is and ought to be the principle, the subject and the
1892-1893   end of all social institutions. Certain societies, such as the family and the civic community, are necessary for the human person. Also helpful are other associations on the national and international levels with due respect for the principle of *subsidiarity*.

403. What is the principle of subsidiarity?

1883-1885   The principle of subsidiarity states that a community of a higher order
1894   should not assume the task belonging to a community of a lower order and deprive it of its authority. It should rather support it in case of need.

404. What else is required for an authentic human society?

Authentic human society requires respect for justice, a just hierarchy of values, and the subordination of material and instinctual dimensions to interior and spiritual ones. In particular, where sin has perverted the social climate, it is necessary to call for the conversion of hearts and for the grace of God to obtain social changes that may really serve each person and the whole person. Charity, which requires and makes possible the practice of justice, is the greatest social commandment. 1886-1889 1895-1896

PARTICIPATION IN SOCIAL LIFE

405. What is the foundation of the authority of society?

Every human community needs a legitimate authority that preserves order and contributes to the realisation of the common good. The foundation of such authority lies in human nature because it corresponds to the order established by God. 1897-1902 1918-1920

406. When is authority exercised in a legitimate way?

Authority is exercised legitimately when it acts for the common good and employs morally licit means to attain it. Therefore, political regimes must be determined by the free decision of their citizens. They should respect the principle of the "rule of law" in which the law, and not the arbitrary will of some, is sovereign. Unjust laws and measures contrary to the moral order are not binding in conscience. 1901-1904 1921-1922

407. What is the common good?

By the common good is meant the sum total of those conditions of social life which allow people as groups and as individuals to reach their proper fulfillment. 1905-1906 1924

408. What is involved in the common good?

The common good involves: respect for and promotion of the fundamental rights of the person, the development of the spiritual and temporal goods of persons and society, and the peace and security of all. 1907-1909 1925

409. Where can one find the most complete realisation of the common good?

The most complete realisation of the common good is found in those political communities which defend and promote the good of their citizens and of intermediate groups without forgetting the universal good of the entire human family. 1910-1912 1927

410. How does one participate in bringing about the common good?

1913-1917   All men and women according to the place and role that they occupy
1926   participate in promoting the common good by respecting just laws and
taking charge of the areas for which they have personal responsibility such
as the care of their own family and the commitment to their own work.
Citizens also should take an active part in public life as far as possible.

SOCIAL JUSTICE

411. How does society ensure social justice?

1928-1933   Society ensures social justice when it respects the dignity and the rights
1943-1944   of the person as the proper end of society itself. Furthermore, society
pursues social justice, which is linked to the common good and to the
exercise of authority, when it provides the conditions that allow associations
and individuals to obtain what is their due.

412. On what is human equality based?

1934-1935   All persons enjoy equal dignity and fundamental rights insofar as they
1945   are created in the image of the one God, are endowed with the same rational
soul, have the same nature and origin, and are called in Christ, the one and
only Saviour, to the same divine beatitude.

413. How are we to view social inequalities?

1936-1938   There are sinful social and economic inequalities which affect millions
1946-1947   of human beings. These inequalities are in open contradiction to the Gospel
and are contrary to justice, to the dignity of persons, and to peace. There are,
however, differences among people caused by various factors which enter
into the plan of God. Indeed, God wills that each might receive what he or
she needs from others and that those endowed with particular talents should
share them with others. Such differences encourage and often oblige people
to the practice of generosity, kindness and the sharing of goods. They also
foster the mutual enrichment of cultures.

414. How is human solidarity manifested?

1939-1942   Solidarity, which springs from human and Christian brotherhood, is
1948   manifested in the first place by the just distribution of goods, by a fair
remuneration for work and by zeal for a more just social order. The *virtue*
of solidarity also practices the sharing of the spiritual goods of faith which
is even more important than sharing material goods.

CHAPTER THREE

GOD'S SALVATION: LAW AND GRACE

THE MORAL LAW

415. What is the moral law?

The moral law is a work of divine Wisdom. It prescribes the ways and the rules of conduct that lead to the promised beatitude and it forbids the ways that turn away from God.

1950-1953
1975-1978

416. In what does the natural moral law consist?

The natural law which is inscribed by the Creator on the heart of every person consists in a participation in the wisdom and the goodness of God. It expresses that original moral sense which enables one to discern by reason the good and the bad. It is universal and immutable and determines the basis of the duties and fundamental rights of the person as well as those of the human community and civil law.

1954-1960
1978-1979

417. Is such a law perceived by everyone?

Because of sin the natural law is not always perceived nor is it recognised by everyone with equal clarity and immediacy.

1960

> *For this reason God "wrote on the tables of the Law what men did not read in their hearts."* (Saint Augustine)

418. What is the relationship between the natural law and the Old Law?

The Old Law is the first stage of revealed Law. It expresses many truths naturally accessible to reason and which are thus affirmed and authenticated in the covenant of salvation. Its moral prescriptions, which are summed up in the Ten Commandments of the Decalogue, lay the foundations of the human vocation, prohibit what is contrary to the love of God and neighbour, and prescribe what is essential to it.

1961-1962
1980

419. What place does the Old Law have in the plan of salvation?

The Old Law permitted one to know many truths which are accessible to reason, showed what must or must not be done and, above all, like a wise tutor, prepared and disposed one for conversion and for the acceptance of the Gospel. However, while being holy, spiritual, and good, the Old Law was still imperfect because in itself it did not give the strength and the grace of the Spirit for its observance.

1963-1964
1982

420. What is the New Law or the Law of the Gospel?

1965-1972   The New Law or the Law of the Gospel, proclaimed and fulfilled by Christ,
1983-1985   is the fullness and completion of the divine law, natural and revealed. It is
summed up in the commandment to love God and neighbour and to love one
another as Christ loved us. It is also an interior reality: the grace of the Holy
Spirit which makes possible such love. It is "the law of freedom" (*Galatians*
1:25) because it inclines us to act spontaneously by the prompting of charity.

> *"The New Law is mainly the same grace of the Holy Spirit which is
> given to believers in Christ."* (Saint Thomas Aquinas)

421. Where does one find the New Law?

1971-1974   The New Law is found in the entire life and preaching of Christ and in
1986   the moral catechesis of the apostles. The Sermon on the Mount is its
principal expression.

GRACE AND JUSTIFICATION

422. What is justification?

1987-1995   Justification is the most excellent work of God's love. It is the merciful and
2017-2020   freely-given act of God which takes away our sins and makes us just and holy
in our whole being. It is brought about by means of the grace of the Holy
Spirit which has been merited for us by the passion of Christ and is given to
us in Baptism. Justification is the beginning of the free response of man, that
is, faith in Christ and of cooperation with the grace of the Holy Spirit.

423. What is the grace that justifies?

1996-1998   That grace is the gratuitous gift that God gives us to make us participants
2005   in his trinitarian life and able to act by his love. It is called *habitual*,
2021   *sanctifying or deifying grace* because it sanctifies and divinises us. It is
supernatural because it depends entirely on God's gratuitous initiative and
surpasses the abilities of the intellect and the powers of human beings. It
therefore escapes our experience.

424. What other kinds of grace are there?

1999-2000   Besides habitual grace, there are actual graces (gifts for specific
2003-2004   circumstances), sacramental graces (gifts proper to each sacrament), special
2023-2024   graces or charisms (gifts that are intended for the common good of the
Church) among which are the graces of state that accompany the exercise of
ecclesial ministries and the responsibilities of life.

425. What is the relationship between grace and human freedom?

Grace precedes, prepares and elicits our free response. It responds to the deep yearnings of human freedom, calls for its cooperation and leads freedom towards its perfection.

2001-2002

426. What is merit?

In general merit refers to the right to recompense for a good deed. With regard to God, we of ourselves are not able to merit anything, having received everything freely from him. However, God gives us the possibility of acquiring merit through union with the love of Christ, who is the source of our merits before God. The merits for good works, therefore must be attributed in the first place to the grace of God and then to the free will of man.

2006-2010
2025-2026

427. What are the goods that we can merit?

Moved by the Holy Spirit, we can merit for ourselves and for others the graces needed for our sanctification and for the attainment of eternal life. Even temporal goods, suitable for us, can be merited in accordance with the plan of God. No one, however, can merit the *initial grace* which is at the origin of conversion and justification.

2010-2011
2027

428. Are all called to Christian holiness?

All the faithful are called to Christian holiness. This is the fullness of Christian life and the perfection of charity and it is brought about by intimate union with Christ and, in him, with the most Holy Trinity. The path to holiness for a Christian goes by way of the cross and will come to its fulfillment in the final resurrection of the just, in which God will be all in all.

2012-2016
2028-2029

THE CHURCH, MOTHER AND TEACHER

429. How does the Church nourish the moral life of a Christian?

The Church is the community in which the Christian receives the Word of God, the teachings of the "Law of Christ" (*Galatians* 6:2), and the grace of the sacraments. Christians are united to the Eucharistic sacrifice of Christ in such a way that their moral life is an act of spiritual worship; and they learn the example of holiness from the Virgin Mary and the lives of the Saints.

2030-2031
2047

430. Why does the Magisterium of the Church act in the field of morality?

2032-2040   It is the duty of the Magisterium of the Church to preach the faith that is
2049-2051   to be believed and put into practice in life. This duty extends even to the
specific precepts of the natural law because their observance is necessary for
salvation.

431. What purpose do the precepts of the Church have?

2041   The five precepts of the Church are meant to guarantee for the faithful
2048   the indispensable minimum in the spirit of prayer, the sacramental life,
moral commitment and growth in love of God and neighbour.

432. What are the precepts of the Church?

2042-2043   They are: 1) to attend Mass on Sundays and other holy days of obligation
and to refrain from work and activities which could impede the
sanctification of those days; 2) to confess one's sins, receiving the
sacrament of Reconciliation at least once each year; 3) to receive the
sacrament of the Eucharist at least during the Easter season; 4) to abstain
from eating meat and to observe the days of fasting established by the
Church; and 5) to help to provide for the material needs of the Church, each
according to his own ability.

433. Why is the Christian moral life indispensable for the proclamation of the Gospel?

2044-2046   Because their lives are conformed to the Lord Jesus, Christians draw
others to faith in the true God, build up the Church, inform the world with
the spirit of the Gospel, and hasten the coming of the Kingdom of God.

THE TEN COMMANDMENTS

A young man addressed this question to Jesus: "Teacher, what good must I do to gain eternal life?" *(Matthew* 19:16). Jesus answered him: "If you wish to enter into life, keep the commandments" and he immediately added: "Come and follow me" (*Matthew* 19:17,21)

Following Jesus implies observing the commandments. The old law has not been abolished; man is rather invited to find it in the person of the divine Master who realised it perfectly in himself, revealed its full meaning, and attested to its perennial value.

The image in this section presents Christ who teaches his disciples in the so-called *Sermon on the Mount* (cf. *Matthew* 5-7). The principal parts of this "sermon" are: the beatitudes, the fulfillment of the old law, the prayer, the *Our Father*, instructions on fasting, and the invitation to the disciples to be the salt of the earth and the light of the world.

The mountain with its elevation above the earth and its closeness to heaven describes a privileged place of encounter with God. Jesus the teacher, seated on the rock as on a favoured chair with the index finger of his right hand pointed to heaven, indicates the divine origin of his words of life and happiness. The scroll which he holds in his left hand signifies the fulfillment of his teaching which he entrusts with confidence to the apostles who are invited to preach the Gospel to all nations, baptising them in the name of the Father, Son, and Holy Spirit.

The twelve apostles who are the crown at the feet of the Master all have a halo to show their loyalty to Christ and the testimony of their holiness in the Church. Only one of them, half hidden at the right, has a black halo, suggesting his infidelity to the good news. The proclamation of the kingdom of God by Jesus was not an empty and inconsistent word but an efficacious and effective action. The story of the paralytic at Capernaum, related by the three synoptics, is significant in this respect:

"He entered a boat, made the crossing, and came into his own town. And there people brought to him a paralytic lying on a stretcher. When Jesus saw their faith, he said to the paralytic, 'Courage, child, your sins are forgiven.' At that some of the scribes said to themselves, 'This man is blaspheming.' Jesus knew what they were thinking and said, 'Why do you harbour evil thoughts? Which is easier, to say 'Your sins are forgiven,' or to say 'Rise and walk'? But that you may know that the Son of Man has authority on earth to forgive sins' - he then said to the paralytic, 'Rise, pick up your stretcher and go home.' He rose and went home" (*Matthew* 9:1-7).

In this episode, the physical cure is nothing other than the visible face of the spiritual miracle of the liberation from sin. Healing and forgiving are typical gestures of the teaching activity of Jesus, the divine Master.

BEATO ANGELICO, *The Sermon on the Mount*, Museum of Saint Mark, Florence.

Exodus 20:2-17	Deuteronomy 5:6-21	A Traditional Catechetical Formula
I am the Lord your God, who brought you out of the land of Egypt, out of the house of bondage.	I am the LORD your God, who brought you out of the land of Egypt, out of the house of bondage.	1. I am the LORD your God.
You shall have no other gods before me. You shall not make for yourself a graven image, or any likeness of anything that is in heaven above, or that is in the earth beneath, or that is in the water under the earth; you shall not bow down to them or serve them; for I the LORD your God am a jealous God, visiting the iniquity of the fathers upon the children to the third and the fourth generation of those who hate me, but showing steadfast love to thousands of those who love me and keep my commandments.	You shall have no other gods before me.	You shall not have strange gods before me.
You shall not take the name of the LORD your God in vain; for the LORD will not hold him guiltless who takes his name in vain.	You shall not take the name of the LORD your God in vain.	2. You shall not take the name of the LORD your God in vain.
Remember the sabbath day, to keep it holy. Six days you shall labour, and do all your work; but the seventh day is a sabbath to the LORD your God; in it	Observe the sabbath day, to keep it holy.	3. Remember to keep holy the LORD's day.

you shall not do any work, you, or your son, or your daughter, your manservant, or your maidservant, or your cattle, or the sojourner who is within your gates; for in six days the LORD made heaven and earth, the sea, and all that is in them, and rested the seventh day; therefore the LORD blessed the sabbath day and hallowed it.

Honour your father and your mother, that your days may be long in the land which the LORD your God gives you.	Honour your father and your mother...	4. Honour your father and your mother.
You shall not kill.	You shall not kill.	5. You shall not kill.
You shall not commit adultery.	Neither shall you commit adultery.	6. You shall not commit adultery.
You shall not steal.	Neither shall you steal.	7. You shall not steal.
You shall not bear false witness against your neighbour.	Neither shall you bear false witness against your neighbour.	8. You shall not bear false witness against your neighbour.
You shall not covet your neighbour's house; you shall not covet your neighbour's wife, or his manservant, or his maidservant, or his ox, or his ass, or anything that is your neighbour's.	Neither shall you covet your neighbour's wife...	9. You shall not covet your neighbour's wife.
	You shall not desire anything that is your neighbour's.	10. You shall not covet your neighbour's goods.

434. "Teacher, what good must I do to have eternal life?" (*Matthew* 19:16).

To the young man who asked this question, Jesus answered, "If you would enter into life, keep the commandments", and then he added, "Come, follow Me" (*Matthew* 19:16-21). To follow Jesus involves keeping the commandments. The law has not been abolished but man is invited to rediscover it in the Person of the divine Master who realised it perfectly in himself, revealed its full meaning and attested to its permanent validity.

2052-2054
2075-2076

435. How did Jesus interpret the Law?

Jesus interpreted the Law in the light of the twofold yet single commandment of love, the fullness of the Law: "You shall love the Lord your God with all your heart and with all your soul and with all your mind. This is the greatest and first commandment. And the second is like it: you shall love your neighbour as yourself. On these two commandments depend all the Law and the Prophets" (*Matthew* 22:37-40).

2055

436. What does "Decalogue" mean?

Decalogue means "ten words" (*Exodus* 34:28). These words sum up the Law given by God to the people of Israel in the context of the Covenant mediated by Moses. This Decalogue, in presenting the commandments of the love of God (the first three) and of one's neighbour (the other seven), traces for the chosen people and for every person in particular the path to a life freed from the slavery of sin.

2056-2057

437. What is the bond between the Decalogue and the Covenant?

The Decalogue must be understood in the light of the Covenant in which God revealed himself and made known his will. In observing the commandments, the people manifested their belonging to God and they answered his initiative of love with thanksgiving.

2058-2063
2077

438. What importance does the Church give to the Decalogue?

The Church, in fidelity to Scripture and to the example of Christ, acknowledges the primordial importance and significance of the Decalogue. Christians are obliged to keep it.

2064-2068

439. Why does the Decalogue constitute an organic unity?

The Ten Commandments form an organic and indivisible whole because each commandment refers to the other commandments and to the entire Decalogue. To break one commandment, therefore, is to violate the entire law.

2069
2079

440. Why does the Decalogue enjoin serious obligations?

2072-2073
2081

It does so because the Decalogue expresses the fundamental duties of man towards God and towards his neighbour.

441. Is it possible to keep the Decalogue?

2074
2082

Yes, because Christ without whom we can do nothing enables us to keep it with the gift of his Spirit and his grace.

CHAPTER ONE

"YOU SHALL LOVE THE LORD YOUR GOD WITH ALL YOUR HEART, WITH ALL YOUR SOUL, AND WITH ALL YOUR MIND"

THE FIRST COMMANDMENT: I AM THE LORD YOUR GOD, YOU SHALL NOT HAVE OTHER GODS BEFORE ME

442. What is implied in the affirmation of God: "I am the Lord your God" (*Exodus* 20:2)?

2083-2094
2133-2134

This means that the faithful must guard and activate the three theological virtues and must avoid sins which are opposed to them. *Faith* believes in God and rejects everything that is opposed to it, such as, deliberate doubt, unbelief, heresy, apostasy, and schism. *Hope* trustingly awaits the blessed vision of God and his help, while avoiding despair and presumption. *Charity* loves God above all things and therefore repudiates indifference, ingratitude, lukewarmness, sloth or spiritual indolence, and that hatred of God which is born of pride.

443. What is the meaning of the words of our Lord, "Adore the Lord your God and worship Him alone" (*Matthew* 4:10)?

2095-2105
2135-2136

These words mean to adore God as the Lord of everything that exists; to render to him the individual and community worship which is his due; to pray to him with sentiments of praise, of thanks, and of supplication; to offer him sacrifices, above all the spiritual sacrifice of one's own life, united with the perfect sacrifice of Christ; and to keep the promises and vows made to him.

444. In what way does a person exercise his or her proper right to worship God in truth and in freedom?

2104-2109
2137

Every person has the right and the moral duty to seek the truth, especially in what concerns God and his Church. Once the truth is known, each person has the right and moral duty to embrace it, to guard it faithfully and to render God authentic worship. At the same time, the dignity of the human person requires that in religious matters no one may be forced to act against conscience nor be restrained, within the just limits of public order, from acting in conformity with conscience, privately or publicly, alone or in association with others.

445. What does God prohibit by his command, "You shall not have other gods before me" (*Exodus* 20:2)?

This commandment forbids:

- *Polytheism* and *idolatry*, which divinises creatures, power, money, or even demons.

- *Superstition* which is a departure from the worship due to the true God and which also expresses itself in various forms of divination, magic, sorcery and spiritism.

- *Irreligion* which is evidenced: in tempting God by word or deed; in sacrilege, which profanes sacred persons or sacred things, above all the Eucharist; and in simony, which involves the buying or selling of spiritual things.

- *Atheism* which rejects the existence of God, founded often on a false conception of human autonomy.

- *Agnosticism* which affirms that nothing can be known about God, and involves indifferentism and practical atheism.

2110-2128
2138-2140

446. Does the commandment of God, "You shall not make for yourself a graven image" (*Exodus* 20:3), forbid the cult of images?

In the Old Testament this commandment forbade any representation of God who is absolutely transcendent. The Christian veneration of sacred images, however, is justified by the incarnation of the Son of God (as taught by the Second Council of Nicea in 787 AD) because such veneration is founded on the mystery of the Son of God made man, in whom the transcendent God is made visible. This does not mean the adoration of an image, but rather the veneration of the one who is represented in it: for example, Christ, the Blessed Virgin Mary, the Angels and the Saints.

2129-2132
2141

447. How does one respect the holiness of the Name of God?

2142-2149   One shows respect for the holy Name of God by blessing it, praising it
2160-2162   and glorifying it. It is forbidden, therefore, to call on the Name of God to
justify a crime. It is also wrong to use the holy Name of God in any
improper way as in *blasphemy* (which by its nature is a grave sin), *curses*,
and *unfaithfulness* to promises made in the Name of God.

448. Why is a false oath forbidden?

2150-2151   It is forbidden because one calls upon God who is Truth itself to be the
2163-2164   witness to a lie.

> *"Do not swear, whether by the Creator or by any creature, except
> truthfully, of necessity and with reverence."* (Saint Ignatius of Loyola)

449. What is perjury?

2152-2155   Perjury is to make a promise under oath with the intention of not keeping
it or to violate a promise made under oath. It is a grave sin against God who
is always faithful to his promises.

THE THIRD COMMANDMENT:
REMEMBER TO KEEP HOLY THE LORD'S DAY

450. Why did God "bless the Sabbath day and declare it sacred" (*Exodus* 20:11)?

2168-2172   God did so because on the Sabbath day one remembers *God's rest* on the
2189   seventh day of creation, and also the liberation of Israel from slavery in
Egypt and the Covenant which God sealed with his people.

451. How did Jesus act in regard to the Sabbath?

2173   Jesus recognised the holiness of the Sabbath day and with divine
authority he gave this law its authentic interpretation: "The Sabbath was
made for man, and not man for the Sabbath" (*Mark* 2:27).

452. For what reason has the Sabbath been changed to Sunday for Christians?

The reason is because Sunday is the day of the Resurrection of Christ. As "the first day of the week" (*Mark* 16:2) it recalls the first creation; and as the "eighth day", which follows the Sabbath, it symbolises the new creation ushered in by the Resurrection of Christ. Thus, it has become for Christians the first of all days and of all feasts. It is the *day of the Lord* in which he with his Passover fulfilled the spiritual truth of the Jewish Sabbath and proclaimed man's eternal rest in God.

2174-2176
2190-2191

453. How does one keep Sunday holy?

Christians keep Sunday and other days of obligation holy by participating in the Eucharist of the Lord and by refraining from those activities which impede the worship of God and disturb the joy proper to the day of the Lord or the necessary relaxation of mind and body. Activities are allowed on the Sabbath which are bound up with family needs or with important social service, provided that they do not lead to habits prejudicial to the holiness of Sunday, to family life and to health.

2177-2185
2192-2193

454. Why is the civil recognition of Sunday as a feast day important?

It is important so that all might be given the real possibility of enjoying sufficient rest and leisure to take care of their religious, familial, cultural and social lives. It is important also to have an opportune time for meditation, for reflection, for silence, for study, and a time to dedicate to good works, particularly for the sick and for the elderly.

2186-2188
2194-2195

CHAPTER TWO

"YOU SHALL LOVE YOUR NEIGHBOUR AS YOURSELF"

THE FOURTH COMMANDMENT:
HONOUR YOUR FATHER AND YOUR MOTHER

455. What does the fourth commandment require?

It commands us to honour and respect our parents and those whom God, for our good, has vested with his authority.

2196-2200
2247-2248

456. What is the nature of the family in the plan of God?

A man and a woman united in marriage form a family together with their children. God instituted the family and endowed it with its fundamental constitution. Marriage and the family are ordered to the good of the spouses

2201-2205
2249

and to the procreation and education of children. Members of the same family establish among themselves personal relationships and primary responsibilities. In Christ the family becomes the *domestic church* because it is a community of faith, of hope, and of charity.

457. What place does the family occupy in society?

2207-2208   The family is the original cell of human society and is, therefore, prior to any recognition by public authority. Family values and principles constitute the foundation of social life. Family life is an initiation into the life of society.

458. What are the duties that society has toward the family?

2209-2213   Society, while respecting the principle of subsidiarity, has the duty to
2250   support and strengthen marriage and the family. Public authority must respect, protect and foster the true nature of marriage and the family, public morality, the rights of parents, and domestic prosperity.

459. What are the duties of children toward their parents?

2214-2220   Children owe respect (filial piety), gratitude, docility and obedience to
2251   their parents. In paying them respect and in fostering good relationships with their brothers and sisters, children contribute to the growth in harmony and holiness in family life in general. Adult children should give their parents material and moral support whenever they find themselves in situations of distress, sickness, loneliness, or old age.

460. What are the duties of parents toward their children?

2221-2231   Parents, in virtue of their participation in the fatherhood of God, have the first responsibility for the education of their children and they are the first heralds of the faith for them. They have the duty to love and respect their children as *persons* and as *children of God* and to provide, as far as is possible, for their physical and spiritual needs. They should select for them a suitable school and help them with prudent counsel in the choice of their profession and their state of life. In particular they have the mission of educating their children in the Christian faith.

461. How are parents to educate their children in the Christian faith?

2252-2253   Parents do this mainly by example, prayer, family catechesis and participation in the life of the Church.

462. Are family bonds an absolute good?

Family ties are important but not absolute, because the first vocation of 2232-2233 a Christian is to follow Jesus and love him: "He who loves father or mother more than me is not worthy of me; whoever loves son or daughter more than me is not worthy of me" (*Matthew* 10:37). Parents must support with joy their children's choice to follow Jesus in whatever state of life, even in the consecrated life or the priestly ministry.

463. How should authority be exercised in the various spheres of civil society?

Authority should always be exercised as a service, respecting 2234-2237 fundamental human rights, a just hierarchy of values, laws, distributive 2254 justice, and the principle of subsidiarity. All those who exercise authority should seek the interests of the community before their own interest and allow their decisions to be inspired by the truth about God, about man and about the world.

464. What are the duties of citizens in regard to civil authorities?

Those subject to authority should regard those in authority as 2238-2241 representatives of God and offer their loyal collaboration for the right 2255 functioning of public and social life. This collaboration includes love and service of one's homeland, the right and duty to vote, payment of taxes, the defence of one's country, and the right to exercise constructive criticism.

465. When is a citizen forbidden to obey civil authorities?

A citizen is obliged in conscience not to obey the laws of civil authorities 2242-2243 when they are contrary to the demands of the moral order: "We must obey 2256 God rather than men" (Acts of the Apostles 5:29).

THE FIFTH COMMANDMENT: YOU SHALL NOT KILL

466. Why must human life be respected?

Human life must be respected because it is *sacred*. From its beginning 2258-2262 human life involves the creative action of God and it remains forever in a 2318-2320 special relationship with the Creator, who is its sole end. It is not lawful for anyone directly to destroy an innocent human being. This is gravely contrary to the dignity of the person and the holiness of the Creator. "Do not slay the innocent and the righteous" (*Exodus* 23:7).

467. Why is the legitimate defence of persons and of society not opposed to this norm?

2263-2265   Because in choosing to legitimately defend oneself one is respecting the right to life (either one's own right to life or that of another) and not choosing to kill. Indeed, for someone responsible for the life of another, legitimate defence can be not only a right but a grave duty, provided only that disproportionate force is not used.

468. What is the purpose of punishment?

2266   A punishment imposed by legitimate public authority has the aim of redressing the disorder introduced by the offence, of defending public order and people's safety, and contributing to the correction of the guilty party.

469. What kind of punishment may be imposed?

2267   The punishment imposed must be proportionate to the gravity of the offence. Given the possibilities which the State now has for effectively preventing crime by rendering one who has committed an offence incapable of doing harm, the cases in which the execution of the offender is an absolute necessity "are very rare, if not practically non-existent" (*Evangelium Vitae*). When non-lethal means are sufficient, authority should limit itself to such means because they better correspond to the concrete conditions of the common good, are more in conformity with the dignity of the human person, and do not remove definitively from the guilty party the possibility of reforming himself.

470. What is forbidden by the fifth commandment?

2268-2283   The fifth commandment forbids as gravely contrary to the moral law:
2321-2326   - *direct and intentional murder* and cooperation in it;
- *direct abortion*, willed as an end or as means, as well as cooperation in it. Attached to this sin is the penalty of excommunication because, from the moment of his or her conception, the human being must be absolutely respected and protected in his integrity;
- *direct euthanasia* which consists in putting an end to the life of the handicapped, the sick, or those near death by an act or by the omission of a required action;
- *suicide* and voluntary cooperation in it, insofar as it is a grave offence against the just love of God, of self, and of neighbour. One's responsibility may be aggravated by the scandal given; one who is psychologically disturbed or is experiencing grave fear may have diminished responsibility.

471. What medical procedures are permitted when death is considered imminent?

When death is considered imminent the ordinary care owed to a sick person cannot be legitimately interrupted. However, it is legitimate to use pain-killers which do not aim at death and to refuse "over-zealous treatment", that is the utilisation of disproportionate medical procedures without reasonable hope of a positive outcome.

2278-2279

472. Why must society protect every embryo?

The inalienable right to life of every human individual from the first moment of conception is a constitutive element of civil society and its legislation. When the State does not place its power at the service of the rights of all and in particular of the more vulnerable, including unborn children, the very foundations of a State based on law are undermined.

2273-2274

473. How does one avoid scandal?

Scandal, which consists in inducing others to do evil, is avoided when we respect the soul and body of the person. Anyone who deliberately leads others to commit serious sins himself commits a grave offence.

2284-2287

474. What duty do we have towards our body?

We must take reasonable *care of our own physical health* and that of others but avoid the *cult of the body* and every kind of excess. Also to be avoided are the use of drugs which cause very serious damage to human health and life, as well as the abuse of food, alcohol, tobacco and medicine.

2288-2291

475. When are scientific, medical, or psychological experiments on human individuals or groups morally legitimate?

They are morally legitimate when they are at the service of the integral good of the person and of society, without disproportionate risks to the life and physical and psychological integrity of the subjects who must be properly informed and consenting.

2292-2295

476. Are the transplant and donation of organs allowed before and after death?

The transplant of organs is morally acceptable with the consent of the donor and without excessive risks to him or her. Before allowing the noble act of organ donation after death, one must verify that the donor is truly dead.

2296

477. What practices are contrary to respect for the bodily integrity of the human person?

2297-2298   They are: kidnapping and hostage-taking, terrorism, torture, violence, and direct sterilisation. Amputations and mutilations of a person are morally permissible only for strictly therapeutic medical reasons.

478. What care must be given to the dying?

2299   The dying have a right to live the last moments of their earthly lives with dignity and, above all, to be sustained with prayer and the sacraments that prepare them to meet the living God.

479. How are the bodies of the deceased to be treated?

2300-2301   The bodies of the departed must be treated with love and respect. Their cremation is permitted provided that it does not demonstrate a denial of faith in the resurrection of the body.

480. What does the Lord ask of every person in regard to peace?

2302-2303   The Lord proclaimed "*Blessed* are the peacemakers" (*Matthew* 5:9). He called for peace of heart and denounced the immorality of anger which is a desire for revenge for some evil suffered. He also denounced hatred which leads one to wish evil on one's neighbour. These attitudes, if voluntary and consented to in matters of great importance, are mortal sins against charity.

481. What is peace in this world?

2304-2305   Peace in this world, which is required for the respect and development of human life, is not simply the absence of war or a balance of power between adversaries. It is "the tranquility of order" (Saint Augustine), "the work of justice" (*Isaiah* 32:17) and the effect of charity. Earthly peace is the image and fruit of the peace of Christ.

482. What is required for earthly peace?

2304
2307-2308   Earthly peace requires the equal distribution and safeguarding of the goods of persons, free communication among human beings, respect for the dignity of persons and peoples, and the assiduous practice of justice and fraternity.

483. When is it morally permitted to use military force?

2307-2310   The use of military force is morally justified when the following conditions are simultaneously present:
- the suffering inflicted by the aggressor must be lasting, grave and certain;
- all other peaceful means must have been shown to be ineffective;
- there are well-founded prospects of success;

- the use of arms, especially given the power of modern weapons of mass destruction, must not produce evils graver than the evil to be eliminated.

484. In danger of war, who has the responsibility for the rigorous evaluation of these conditions?

This responsibility belongs to the prudential judgment of government officials who also have the right to impose on citizens the obligation of national defence. The personal right to conscientious objection makes an exception to this obligation which should then be carried out by another form of service to the human community.

2309

485. In case of war, what does the moral law require?

Even during a war the moral law always remains valid. It requires the humane treatment of non-combatants, wounded soldiers and prisoners of war. Deliberate actions contrary to the law of nations, and the orders that command such actions are crimes, which blind obedience does not excuse. Acts of mass destruction must be condemned and likewise the extermination of peoples or ethnic minorities, which are most grievous sins. One is morally bound to resist the orders that command such acts.

2312-2314
2328

486. What must be done to avoid war?

Because of the evils and injustices that all war brings with it, we must do everything reasonably possible to avoid it. To this end it is particularly important to avoid: the accumulation and sale of arms which are not regulated by the legitimate authorities; all forms of economic and social injustice; ethnic and religious discrimination; envy, mistrust, pride and the spirit of revenge. Everything done to overcome these and other disorders contributes to building up peace and avoiding war.

2315-2317
2327-2330

THE SIXTH COMMANDMENT: YOU SHALL NOT COMMIT ADULTERY

487. What responsibility do human persons have in regard to their own sexual identity?

God has created human beings as male and female, equal in personal dignity, and has called them to a vocation of love and of communion. Everyone should accept his or her identity as male or female, recognising its importance for the whole of the person, its specificity and complementarity.

2331-2336
2392-2393

488. What is chastity?

Chastity means the positive integration of sexuality within the person. Sexuality becomes truly human when it is integrated in a correct way into

2337-2338

the relationship of one person to another. Chastity is a moral virtue, a gift of God, a grace, and a fruit of the Holy Spirit.

489. What is involved in the virtue of chastity?

2339-2341   The virtue of chastity involves an apprenticeship in self-mastery as an expression of human freedom directed towards self-giving. An integral and continuing formation, which is brought about in stages, is necessary to achieve this goal.

490. What are the means that aid the living of chastity?

2340-2347   There are many means at one's disposal: the grace of God, the help of the sacraments, prayer, self-knowledge, the practice of an asceticism adapted to various situations, the exercise of the moral virtues, especially the virtue of temperance which seeks to have the passions guided by reason.

491. In what way is everyone called to live chastity?

2348-2350   As followers of Christ, the model of all chastity, all the baptised are
2394   called to live chastely in keeping with their particular states of life. Some profess virginity or consecrated celibacy which enables them to give themselves to God alone with an undivided heart in a remarkable manner. Others, if they are married live in conjugal chastity, or if unmarried practise chastity in continence.

492. What are the principal sins against chastity?

2351-2359   Grave sins against chastity differ according to their object: adultery,
2396   masturbation, fornication, pornography, prostitution, rape, and homosexual acts. These sins are expressions of the vice of lust. These kinds of acts committed against the physical and moral integrity of minors become even more grave.

493. Although it says only "you shall not commit adultery" why does the sixth commandment forbid all sins against chastity?

2336   Although the biblical text of the Decalogue reads "you shall not commit adultery" (*Exodus* 20:14), the Tradition of the Church comprehensively follows the moral teachings of the Old and New Testaments and considers the sixth commandment as encompassing all sins against chastity.

494. What is the responsibility of civil authority in regard to chastity?

2354   Insofar as it is bound to promote respect for the dignity of the person, civil authority should seek to create an environment conducive to the practice of chastity. It should also enact suitable legislation to prevent the spread of the grave offences against chastity mentioned above, especially in order to protect minors and those who are the weakest members of society.

495. What are the goods of conjugal love to which sexuality is ordered?

The goods of conjugal love, which for those who are baptised is sanctified by the sacrament of Matrimony, are unity, fidelity, indissolubility, and an openness to the procreation of life. 2360-2361
2397-2398

496. What is the meaning of the conjugal act?

The conjugal act has a twofold meaning: unitive (the mutual self-giving of the spouses) and procreative (an openness to the transmission of life). No one may break the inseparable connection which God has established between these two meanings of the conjugal act by excluding one or the other of them. 2362-2367

497. When is it moral to regulate births?

The regulation of births, which is an aspect of responsible fatherhood and motherhood, is objectively morally acceptable when it is pursued by the spouses without external pressure; when it is practiced not out of selfishness but for serious reasons; and with methods that conform to the objective criteria of morality, that is, periodic continence and use of the infertile periods. 2368-2369
2399

498. What are immoral means of birth control?

Every action - for example, direct sterilisation or contraception - is intrinsically immoral which (either in anticipation of the conjugal act, in its accomplishment or in the development of its natural consequences) proposes, as an end or as a means, to hinder procreation. 2370-2372

499. Why are artificial insemination and artificial fertilization immoral?

They are immoral because they dissociate procreation from the act with which the spouses give themselves to each other and so introduce the domination of technology over the origin and destiny of the human person. Furthermore, heterologous insemination and fertilisation with the use of techniques that involve a person other than the married couple infringe upon the right of a child to be born of a father and mother known to him, bound to each other by marriage and having the exclusive right to become parents only through each another. 2373-2377

500. How should children be considered?

2378   A child is a *gift of God*, the supreme gift of marriage. There is no such thing as a right to have children (e.g. "a child at any cost"). But a child does have the right to be the fruit of the conjugal act of its parents as well as the right to be respected as a person from the moment of conception.

501. What can spouses do when they do not have children?

2379   Should the gift of a child not be given to them, after exhausting all legitimate medical options, spouses can show their generosity by way of foster care or adoption or by performing meaningful services for others. In this way they realise a precious spiritual fruitfulness.

502. What are the offences against the dignity of marriage?

2380-2391   These are: adultery, divorce, polygamy, incest, free unions (cohabitation,
2400   concubinage), and sexual acts before or outside of marriage.

THE SEVENTH COMMANDMENT: YOU SHALL NOT STEAL

503. What is set forth by the seventh commandment?

2401-2402   The seventh commandment requires respect for the universal destination and distribution of goods and the private ownership of them, as well as respect for persons, their property, and the integrity of creation. The Church also finds in this commandment the basis for her social doctrine which involves the correct way of acting in economic, social and political life, the right and the duty of human labour, justice and solidarity among nations, and love for the poor.

504. Under what conditions does the right to private property exist?

2403   The right to private property exists provided the property is acquired or received in a just way and that the universal destination of goods for the satisfaction of the basic needs of all takes precedence.

505. What is the purpose of private property?

2404-2406   The purpose of private property is to guarantee the freedom and dignity of individual persons by helping them to meet the basic needs of those in their charge and also of others who are in need.

506. What does the seventh commandment require?

The seventh commandment requires respect for the goods of others through the practice of justice and charity, temperance and solidarity. In particular it requires *respect for promises made and contracts agreed to, reparation for injustice* committed and restitution of stolen goods, and respect for the *integrity of creation* by the prudent and moderate use of the mineral, vegetable, and animal resources of the universe with special attention to those species which are in danger of extinction.

2407
2450-2451

507. What attitude should people have towards animals?

People must treat animals with kindness as creatures of God and avoid both excessive love for them and an indiscriminate use of them especially by scientific experiments that go beyond reasonable limits and entail needless suffering for the animals.

2416-2418
2457

508. What is forbidden by the seventh commandment?

Above all, the seventh commandment forbids theft, which is the taking or using of another's property against the reasonable will of the owner. This can be done also by paying unjust wages; by speculation on the value of goods in order to gain an advantage to the detriment of others; or by the forgery of cheques or invoices. Also forbidden is tax evasion or business fraud; willfully damaging private or public property; usury; corruption; the private abuse of common goods; work deliberately done poorly; and waste.

2408-2413
2453-2455

509. What is the content of the social doctrine of the Church?

The social doctrine of the Church is an organic development of the truth of the Gospel about the dignity of the human person and his social dimension offering principles for reflection, criteria for judgment, and norms and guidelines for action.

2419-2423

510. When does the Church intervene in social areas?

The Church intervenes by making a moral judgment about economic and social matters when the fundamental rights of the person, the common good, or the salvation of souls requires it.

2420
2458

511. How should social and economic life be pursued?

It should be pursued according to its own proper methods within the sphere of the moral order, at the service of the whole human being and of the entire human community in keeping with social justice. Social and economic life should have the human person as its author, centre, and goal.

2459

512. What would be opposed to the social doctrine of the Church?

2424-2425   Opposed to the social doctrine of the Church are economic and social systems that sacrifice the basic rights of persons or that make profit their exclusive norm or ultimate end. For this reason the Church rejects the ideologies associated in modern times with communism or with atheistic and totalitarian forms of socialism. But in the practice of capitalism the Church also rejects self-centred individualism and an absolute primacy of the laws of the marketplace over human labour.

513. What is the meaning of work?

2426-2428   Work is both a duty and a right through which human beings collaborate
2460-2461   with God the Creator. Indeed, by working with commitment and competence we fulfill the potential inscribed in our nature, honour the Creator's gifts and the talents received from him, provide for ourselves and for our families, and serve the human community. Furthermore, by the grace of God, work can be a means of sanctification and collaboration with Christ for the salvation of others.

514. To what type of work does every person have a right?

2429   Access to secure and honest employment must be open to all without
2433-2434   unjust discrimination and with respect for free economic initiative and fair compensation.

515. What responsibility does the State have in regard to labour?

2431   It is the role of the State to guarantee individual freedom and private property, as well as a stable currency and efficient public services. It is also the State's responsibility to oversee and direct the exercise of human rights in the economic sector. According to circumstances, society must help citizens to find work.

516. What is the task of business management?

2432   Business managers are responsible for the economic and ecological effects of their operations. They must consider the good of persons and not only the increase of profits, even though profits are necessary to assure investments, the future of the business, employment, and the good progress of economic life.

517. What are the duties of workers?

2435   They must carry out their work in a conscientious way with competence and dedication, seeking to resolve any controversies with dialogue.

Recourse to a non-violent strike is morally legitimate when it appears to be the necessary way to obtain a proportionate benefit and it takes into account the common good.

518. How is justice and solidarity among nations brought about?

On the international level, all nations and institutions must carry out their work in solidarity and subsidiarity for the purpose of eliminating or at least reducing poverty, the inequality of resources and economic potential, economic and social injustices, the exploitation of persons, the accumulation of debts by poor countries, and the perverse mechanisms that impede the development of the less advanced countries. 2437-2441

519. In what way do Christians participate in political and social life?

The lay faithful take part directly in political and social life by animating temporal realities with a Christian spirit and collaborating with all as authentic witnesses of the Gospel and agents of peace and justice. 2442

520. By what is love for the poor inspired?

Love for the poor is inspired by the Gospel of the Beatitudes and by the example of Jesus in his constant concern for the poor. Jesus said, "Whatever you have done to the least of my brethren, you have done to me" (*Matthew* 25:40). Love for the poor shows itself through the struggle against material poverty and also against the many forms of cultural, moral, and religious poverty. The spiritual and corporal works of mercy and the many charitable institutions formed throughout the centuries are a concrete witness to the preferential love for the poor which characterises the disciples of Jesus. 2443-2449 2462-2463

THE EIGHTH COMMANDMENT:
YOU SHALL NOT BEAR FALSE WITNESS AGAINST YOUR NEIGHBOUR

521. What is one's duty towards the truth?

Every person is called to sincerity and truthfulness in acting and speaking. Everyone has the duty to seek the truth, to adhere to it and to order one's whole life in accordance with its demands. In Jesus Christ the whole of God's truth has been made manifest. He is "*the truth*". Those who follow him live in the Spirit of truth and guard against duplicity, dissimulation, and hypocrisy. 2464-2470 2504

522. How does one bear witness to the truth?

A Christian must bear witness to the truth of the Gospel in every field of his activity, both public and private, and also if necessary, with the 2471-2474 2505-2506 sacrifice of his very life. Martyrdom is the supreme witness given to the truth of the faith.

523. What is forbidden by the eighth commandment?

2475-2487
2507-2509
The eighth commandment forbids:

- *false witness*, *perjury*, and *lying*, the gravity of which is measured by the truth it deforms, the circumstances, the intentions of the one who lies, and the harm suffered by its victims;

- *rash judgment*, *slander*, *defamation* and *calumny* which diminish or destroy the good reputation and honour to which every person has a right;

- *flattery*, *adulation*, or *complaisance*, especially if directed to serious sins or towards the achievement of illicit advantages.

A sin committed against truth demands reparation if it has caused harm to others.

524. What is required by the eighth commandment?

2488-2492
2510-2511
The eighth commandment requires respect for the truth accompanied by the discretion of charity in the field of *communication* and the *imparting of information*, where the personal and common good, the protection of privacy and the danger of scandal must all be taken into account; in respecting *professional secrets* which must be kept, save in exceptional cases for grave and proportionate reasons; and also in respecting *confidences* given under the seal of secrecy.

525. How is one to use the means of social communication?

2493-2499
2512
The information provided by the media must be at the service of the common good. Its content must be true and - within the limits of justice and charity - also complete. Furthermore, information must be communicated honestly and properly with scrupulous respect for moral laws and the legitimate rights and dignity of the person.

526. What relationship exists between truth, beauty and sacred art?

2500-2503
2513
The truth is beautiful, carrying in itself the splendour of spiritual beauty. In addition to the expression of the truth in words there are other complementary expressions of the truth, most specifically in the beauty of artistic works. These are the fruit both of talents given by God and of human effort. *Sacred art* by being true and beautiful should evoke and glorify the mystery of God made visible in Christ, and lead to the adoration and love of God, the Creator and Saviour, who is the surpassing, invisible Beauty of Truth and Love.

THE NINTH COMMANDMENT:
YOU SHALL NOT COVET YOUR NEIGHBOUR'S WIFE

527. What is required by the ninth commandment?

The ninth commandment requires that one overcome carnal concupiscence in thought and in desire. The struggle against such concupiscence entails purifying the heart and practising the virtue of temperance.

2514-2516
2528-2530

528. What is forbidden by the ninth commandment?

The ninth commandment forbids cultivating thoughts and desires connected to actions forbidden by the sixth commandment.

2517-2519
2531-2532

529. How does one reach purity of heart?

In the battle against disordered desires the baptised person is able, by the grace of God, to achieve purity of heart through the virtue and gift of chastity, through purity of intention, purity of vision (both exterior and interior), discipline of the imagination and of feelings and by prayer.

2520

530. What are the other requirements for purity?

Purity requires *modesty* which, while protecting the intimate centre of the person, expresses the sensitivity of chastity. It guides how one looks at others and behaves towards them in conformity with the dignity of persons and their communion. Purity frees one from wide-spread eroticism and avoids those things which foster morbid curiosity. Purity also requires a *purification of the social climate* by means of a constant struggle against moral permissiveness which is founded on an erroneous conception of human freedom.

2521-2527
2533

THE TENTH COMMANDMENT: YOU SHALL NOT COVET YOUR NEIGHBOUR'S POSSESSIONS

531. What is required and what is forbidden by the tenth commandment?

This commandment, which completes the preceding commandment, requires an interior attitude of respect for the property of others and forbids *greed*, *unbridled covetousness* for the goods of others, and *envy* which is the sadness one experiences at the sight of another's goods and the immoderate desire to acquire them for oneself.

2534-2540
2551-2554

532. What does Jesus call for in poverty of spirit?

2544-2547
2556
Jesus calls his disciples to prefer him to everything and everyone. Detachment from riches - in the spirit of evangelical poverty - and self-abandonment to divine providence free us from anxiety about the future and prepare us for the blessedness of the "poor in spirit, for theirs is the kingdom of heaven" (*Mathew* 5:3).

533. What is the greatest human desire?

2548-2550
2557
The greatest desire of the human person is to see God. "I want to see God" is the cry of our whole being. We realise our true and full happiness in the vision and beatitude of the One who created us out of love and draws us to himself with infinite love.

"Whoever sees God has obtained all the goods of which he can conceive." (Saint Gregory of Nyssa)

This icon calls to mind the biblical account of Pentecost:

"When the time for Pentecost was fulfilled, they were all in one place together. And suddenly there came from the sky a noise like a strong driving wind and it filled the entire house in which they were. Then there appeared to them tongues as of fire which parted and came to rest on each one of them. And they were all filled with the Holy Spirit and began to speak in different tongues as the Spirit enabled them to proclaim" (*Acts* 2:1-4).

In this image there comes from the dove, a symbol of the Holy Spirit, a cone of intense light which wraps itself around Mary and the apostles. This is the light which illumines the minds of the apostles and gives them the gifts of knowledge, wisdom, and understanding of divine things along with the gifts of piety, fortitude, counsel, and fear of the Lord.

Tongues of fire rest on their heads to show the fullness of God's love which will move them to be preachers of the Gospel to all the nations. This abundance of grace will actually enable the apostles to be understood by all for the language of charity is universal and accessible to all.

To the barrier which the different languages created among people Pentecost counterpoises the remedy of unity among the nations.

Mary, mother of the Church, the Queen of the apostles, and the perfect "pray-er", is the dominant figure at the centre of the icon. It is in the love of the Holy Spirit that the faithful can raise their filial prayer to God in accord with the words of the apostle:

"As proof that you are children, God sent the spirit of his Son into our hearts, crying out, 'Abba, Father!'" (*Galatians* 4:6).

Coptic Icon of Pentecost.

PART FOUR

CHRISTIAN PRAYER

PRAYER IN
THE CHRISTIAN LIFE

All times are good for prayer. The Church, however, proposes special times to the faithful to stress and nurture continual prayer: morning and evening prayer, prayers before and after meals, the Liturgy of the Hours, the Sunday Eucharist, the Rosary, and the feasts of the liturgical year.

This icon portrays some of the major feasts of the liturgical year which mark the prayer of the Church. The representation of the paschal mystery, the Resurrection and the Ascension of Jesus into heaven, is the dominant figure at the centre of the icon. This solemn feast is the summit of liturgical prayer and from it all the other feasts, both those of Jesus and Mary, draw their meaning and saving efficacy.

Icon of the Principal Liturgical Feasts.

534. What is prayer?

Prayer is the raising of one's mind and heart to God, or the petition of good things from him in accord with his will. It is always the gift of God who comes to encounter man. Christian prayer is the personal and living relationship of the children of God with their Father who is infinitely good, with his Son Jesus Christ, and with the Holy Spirit who dwells in their hearts.

2558-2565
2590

CHAPTER ONE

THE REVELATION OF PRAYER

535. Why is there a universal call to prayer?

Because through creation God first calls every being from nothingness. Even after the Fall man continues to be capable of recognising his Creator and retains a desire for the One who has called him into existence. All religions, and the whole history of salvation in particular, bear witness to this human desire for God. It is God first of all, however, who ceaselessly draws every person to the mysterious encounter known as prayer.

2566-2567

THE REVELATION OF PRAYER IN THE OLD TESTAMENT

536. How is Abraham a model of prayer?

Abraham is a model of prayer because he walked in the presence of God, heard and obeyed him. His prayer was a battle of faith because he continued to believe in the fidelity of God even in times of trial. Besides, after having received in his own tent the visit of the Lord who confided his plan to him, Abraham dared to intercede for sinners with bold confidence.

2570-2573
2592

537. How did Moses pray?

The prayer of Moses was typical of contemplative prayer. God, who called to Moses from the burning bush, lingered in conversation with him often and at length, "face-to-face, like a man with his friend" (*Exodus* 33:11). In this intimacy with God, Moses attained the strength to intercede tenaciously for his people: his prayer thus prefigured the intercession of the one mediator, Christ Jesus.

2574-2577
2593

538. In the Old Testament, what relationship do the king and the temple have to prayer?

The prayer of the people of God developed in the shadow of the dwelling place of God - the Ark of the Covenant, then the Temple - under the

2578-2580
2594

guidance of their shepherds. Among them there was David, the King "after God's own heart," the shepherd who prayed for his people. His prayer was a model for the prayer of the people because it involved clinging to the divine promise and a trust filled with love for the One who is the only King and Lord.

539. What is the role of prayer in the mission of the prophets?

2581-2584   The prophets drew from prayer the light and strength to exhort the people to faith and to conversion of heart. They entered into great intimacy with God and interceded for their brothers and sisters to whom they proclaimed what they had seen and heard from the Lord. Elijah was the father of the prophets, of those who sought the face of God. On Mount Carmel he achieved the return of the people to the faith, thanks to the intervention of God to whom he prayed: "Answer me, O Lord, answer me!" (1 *Kings* 18:37).

540. What is the importance of the Psalms in prayer?

2579
2585-2589
2596-2597   The Psalms are the summit of prayer in the Old Testament: the Word of God become the prayer of man. Inseparably both personal and communal, and inspired by the Holy Spirit, this prayer sings of God's marvelous deeds in creation and in the history of salvation. Christ prayed the Psalms and brought them to fulfillment. Thus they remain an essential and permanent element of the prayer of the Church suited to people of every condition and time.

PRAYER IS FULLY REVEALED AND REALISED IN JESUS

541. From whom did Jesus learn how to pray?

2599
2620   Jesus, with his human heart, learned how to pray from his mother and from the Jewish tradition. But his prayer sprang from a more secret source because he is the eternal Son of God who in his holy humanity offers his perfect filial prayer to his Father.

542. When did Jesus pray?

2600-2604
2620   The Gospel often shows Jesus at prayer. We see him draw apart to pray in solitude, even at night. He prays before the decisive moments of his mission or that of his apostles. In fact, all his life is a prayer because he is in a constant communion of love with the Father.

543. How did Jesus pray during his passion?

2605-2606
2620   The prayer of Jesus during his agony in the garden of Gethsemane and his last words on the cross reveal the depth of his filial prayer. Jesus brings to completion the loving plan of the Father and takes upon himself all the

anguish of humanity and all the petitions and intercessions of the history of salvation. He presents them to the Father who accepts them and answers them beyond all hope by raising his Son from the dead.

544. How does Jesus teach us to pray?

Jesus teaches us to pray not only with the *Our Father* but also when he prays. In this way he teaches us, in addition to the content, the dispositions necessary for every true prayer: purity of heart that seeks the Kingdom and forgives one's enemies, bold and filial faith that goes beyond what we feel and understand, and watchfulness that protects the disciple from temptation.

2608-2614 2621

545. Why is our prayer efficacious?

Our prayer is efficacious because it is united in faith with the prayer of Jesus. In him Christian prayer becomes a communion of love with the Father. In this way we can present our petitions to God and be heard: "Ask and you will receive that your joy may be full" (*John* 16:24).

2615-2616

546. How did the Virgin Mary pray?

Mary's prayer was characterised by faith and by the generous offering of her whole being to God. The Mother of Jesus is also the new Eve, the "Mother of all the living". She prays to Jesus for the needs of all people.

2617, 2618 2622, 2674 2679

547. Is there a prayer of Mary in the Gospel?

Along with the prayer of Mary at Cana in Galilee, the Gospel gives us the *Magnificat* (*Luke* 1:46-55) which is the song both of the Mother of God and of the Church, the joyous thanksgiving that rises from the hearts of the poor because their hope is met by the fulfillment of the divine promises.

2619

PRAYER IN THE AGE OF THE CHURCH

548. How did the first Christian community in Jerusalem pray?

At the beginning of the *Acts of the Apostles* it is written that in the first community of Jerusalem, educated in the life of prayer by the Holy Spirit, the faithful "devoted themselves to the teaching of the apostles and to the communal life, to the breaking of the bread, and to the prayers" (*Acts* 2:42).

2623-2624

549. How does the Holy Spirit intervene in the Church's prayer?

The Holy Spirit, the interior Master of Christian prayer, forms the Church in the life of prayer and allows her to enter ever more deeply into

2623, 2625

contemplation of and union with the unfathomable mystery of Christ. The forms of prayer expressed in the apostolic and canonical writings remain normative for Christian prayer.

550. What are the essential forms of Christian prayer?

2643-2644   They are blessing and adoration, the prayer of petition and intercession, thanksgiving and praise. The Eucharist contains and expresses all the forms of prayer.

551. What is "blessing"?

2626-2627   The prayer of blessing is man's response to God's gifts: we bless the
2645   Almighty who first blesses us and fills us with his gifts.

552. How can adoration be defined?

2628   Adoration is the humble acknowledgement by human beings that they are creatures of the thrice-holy Creator.

553. What are the different forms of the prayer of petition?

2629-2633   It can be a petition for pardon or also a humble and trusting petition for
2646   all our needs either spiritual or material. The first thing to ask for, however, is the coming of the Kingdom.

554. In what does the prayer of intercession consist?

2634-2636   Intercession consists in asking on behalf of another. It conforms us and
2647   unites us to the prayer of Jesus who intercedes with the Father for all, especially sinners. Intercession must extend even to one's enemies.

555. When is thanksgiving given to God?

2637-2638   The Church gives thanks to God unceasingly, above all in celebrating
2648   the Eucharist in which Christ allows her to participate in his own thanksgiving to the Father. For the Christian every event becomes a reason for giving thanks.

556. What is the prayer of praise?

2639-2643   Praise is that form of prayer which recognises most immediately that
2649   God is God. It is a completely disinterested prayer: it sings God's praise for his own sake and gives him glory simply because he is.

CHAPTER TWO

THE TRADITION OF PRAYER

557. What is the importance of Tradition in regard to prayer?

In the Church it is through living Tradition that the Holy Spirit teaches   2650-2651
the children of God how to pray. In fact prayer cannot be reduced to the
spontaneous outpouring of an interior impulse; rather it implies
contemplation, study and a grasp of the spiritual realities one experiences.

AT THE WELLSPRINGS OF PRAYER

558. What are the sources of Christian prayer?

They are: the *Word of God* which gives us "the surpassing knowledge"   2652-2662
of Christ (*Philippians* 3:8); the *Liturgy of the Church* that proclaims, makes
present and communicates the mystery of salvation; the *theological virtues*;
and *everyday situations* because in them we can encounter God.

> *"I love you, Lord, and the only grace I ask is to love you eternally.*
> *... My God, if my tongue cannot say in every moment that I love you,*
> *I want my heart to repeat it to you as often as I draw breath."*
> (The Curé of Ars, Saint John Mary Vianney)

THE WAY OF PRAYER

559. In the Church are there different ways of praying?

In the Church there are various ways of praying that are tied to different   2663
historical, social and cultural contexts. The Magisterium of the Church has
the task of discerning the fidelity of these ways of praying to the tradition of
apostolic faith. It is for pastors and catechists to explain their meaning
which is always related to Jesus Christ.

560. What is the way of our prayer?

The way of our prayer is Christ because prayer is directed to God our   2664
Father but reaches him only if we pray - at least implicitly - in the name of   2680-2681
Jesus. His humanity is in effect the only way by which the Holy Spirit
teaches us to pray to our Father. Therefore liturgical prayers conclude with
the formula: "Through our Lord Jesus Christ."

561. What is the role of the Holy Spirit in prayer?

2670-2672
2680-2681

Since the Holy Spirit is the interior Master of Christian prayer and "we do not know how to pray as we ought" (*Romans* 8:26), the Church exhorts us to invoke him and implore him on every occasion: "Come, Holy Spirit!"

562. How is Christian prayer Marian?

2673-2679
2682

Because of her singular cooperation with the action of the Holy Spirit, the Church loves to pray to Mary and with Mary, the perfect "pray-er", and to "magnify" and invoke the Lord with her. Mary in effect shows us the "Way" who is her Son, the one and only Mediator.

563. How does the Church pray to Mary?

2676-2678
2682

Above all with the *Hail Mary*, the prayer with which the Church asks the intercession of the Virgin. Other Marian prayers are the *Rosary*, the *Akathistos* hymn, the *Paraclesis*, and the hymns and canticles of diverse Christian traditions.

GUIDES FOR PRAYER

564. How are the saints guides for prayer?

2683-2684
2692-2693

The saints are our models of prayer. We also ask them to intercede before the Holy Trinity for us and for the whole world. Their intercession is their most exalted service to God's plan. In the communion of saints, throughout the history of the Church, there have developed different types of *spiritualities* that teach us how to live and to practice the way of prayer.

565. Who can educate us in prayer?

2685-2690
2694-2695

The Christian family is the first place of education in prayer. Daily family prayer is particularly recommended because it is the first witness to the life of prayer in the Church. Catechesis, prayer groups, and "spiritual direction" constitute a school of and a help to prayer.

566. What places are conducive to prayer?

2691
2696

One can pray anywhere but the choice of an appropriate place is not a matter of indifference when it comes to prayer. The church is the proper place for liturgical prayer and Eucharistic adoration. Other places also help one to pray, such as a "prayer corner" at home, a monastery or a shrine.

CHAPTER THREE
THE LIFE OF PRAYER

567. What times are more suitable for prayer?

Any time is suitable for prayer but the Church proposes to the faithful certain rhythms of praying intended to nourish continual prayer: morning and evening prayer, prayer before and after meals, the Liturgy of the Hours, Sunday Eucharist, the Rosary, and feasts of the liturgical year.

2697-2698
2720

> *"We must remember God more often than we draw breath."*
> (Saint Gregory of Nazianzus)

568. What are the expressions of the life of prayer?

Christian tradition has preserved three forms for expressing and living prayer: vocal prayer, meditation, and contemplative prayer. The feature common to all of them is the recollection of the heart.

2697-2699

EXPRESSIONS OF PRAYER

569. How can vocal prayer be described?

Vocal prayer associates the body with the interior prayer of the heart. Even the most interior prayer, however, cannot dispense with vocal prayer. In any case it must always spring from a personal faith. With the *Our Father* Jesus has taught us a perfect form of vocal prayer.

2700-2704
2722

570. What is meditation?

Meditation is a prayerful reflection that begins above all in the Word of God in the Bible. Meditation engages thought, imagination, emotion and desire in order to deepen our faith, convert our heart and fortify our will to follow Christ. It is a first step towards the union of love with our Lord.

2705-2708
2723

571. What is contemplative prayer?

Contemplative prayer is a simple gaze upon God in silence and love. It is a gift of God, a moment of pure faith during which the one praying seeks Christ, surrenders himself to the loving will of the Father, and places his being under the action of the Holy Spirit. Saint Teresa of Avila defines contemplative prayer as the intimate sharing of friendship, "in which time is frequently taken to be alone with God who we know loves us."

2709-2719
2724
2739-2741

THE BATTLE OF PRAYER

572. Why is prayer a "battle"?

2725   Prayer is a gift of grace but it always presupposes a determined response on our part because those who pray "battle" against themselves, their surroundings, and especially the Tempter who does all he can to turn them away from prayer. The battle of prayer is inseparable from progress in the spiritual life. We pray as we live because we live as we pray.

573. Are there objections to prayer?

2726-2728   Along with erroneous notions of prayer, many think they do not have the
2752-2753   time to pray or that praying is useless. Those who pray can be discouraged in the face of difficulties and apparent lack of success. Humility, trust and perseverance are necessary to overcome these obstacles.

574. What are the difficulties in prayer?

2729-2733   *Distraction* is a habitual difficulty in our prayer. It takes our
2754-2755   attention away from God and can also reveal what we are attached to. Our heart therefore must humbly turn to the Lord. Prayer is often affected by *dryness*. Overcoming this difficulty allows us to cling to the Lord in faith, even without any feeling of consolation. *Acedia* is a form of spiritual laziness due to relaxed vigilance and a lack of custody of the heart.

575. How may we strengthen our filial trust?

2734-2741   Filial trust is tested when we think we are not heard. We must therefore
2756   ask ourselves if we think God is truly a Father whose will we seek to fulfill, or simply a means to obtain what we want. If our prayer is united to that of Jesus, we know that he gives us much more than this or that gift. We receive the Holy Spirit who transforms our heart.

576. Is it possible to pray always?

2742-2745   Praying is always possible because the time of the Christian is the time
2757   of the risen Christ who remains "with us always" (*Matthew* 28:20). Prayer and Christian life are therefore inseparable:

"It is possible to offer frequent and fervent prayer even at the market place or strolling alone. It is possible also in your place of business, while buying or selling, or even while cooking."
(Saint John Chrysostom)

577. What is the prayer of the *Hour* of Jesus?

It is called the priestly prayer of Jesus at the Last Supper. Jesus, the High Priest of the New Covenant, addresses it to his Father when the *hour* of his sacrifice, the *hour* of his "passing over" to him is approaching.

2604
2746-2751
2758

THE LORD'S PRAYER:
"OUR FATHER"

Our Father

Our Father who art in heaven,
hallowed be thy name.
Thy kingdom come.
Thy will be done on earth,
as it is in heaven.
Give us this day our daily bread,
and forgive us our trespasses,
as we forgive those who trespass
against us,
and lead us not into temptation,
but deliver us from evil.

Pater Noster

Pater noster qui es in cælis,
sanctificétur Nomen Tuum;
advéniat Regnum Tuum;
fiat volúntas Tua,
sicut in cælo, et in terra.
Panem nostrum cotidiánum da nobis
hódie; et dimítte nobis débita nostra,
sicut et nos dimíttimus
debitóribus nostris;
et ne nos indúcas in tentatiónem;
sed líbera nos a Malo.

"He was praying in a certain place and when he had finished, one of his disciples said to him 'Lord, teach us to pray'" (*Luke* 11:1). Jesus responded by teaching them the *Our Father*.

The disciples, who had experience with Jewish prayer at the time, were greatly struck by the singular character of the prayer of their Master. Jesus actually was in continual prayer (cf. *Luke* 5:16). The most important moments of his life were accompanied by prayer. Jesus prayed at his baptism in the Jordan (*Luke* 3:21), before calling the apostles (*Luke* 6:12), and before his Transfiguration (*Luke* 9:28). He prayed for the faith of Peter (*Luke* 22:31-32) and for the sending of the Holy Spirit (*John* 14:15-17). He prayed before raising Lazarus (*John* 11:41) and at his triumphant entry into Jerusalem (*John* 12:27). He prayed to his Father for his own glorification at the Last Supper (*John* 17:1-5), for his disciples (*John* 17:6-19), and for all believers (*John* 17:20-26). He prayed before his passion (*Luke* 22:39-46) and at the moment of his death he prayed for his enemies (*Luke* 23:24).

The prayer of Jesus was addressed to the Father in a dialogue of obedience which gave life to his mission: "My food is to do the will of the one who sent me and to finish his work" (*John* 4:34). This intimate communion with the Father is the source of joy and praise: "I give praise to you, Father, Lord of heaven and earth... All things have been handed over to me by my Father. No one knows the Son except the Father and no one knows the Father except the Son and anyone to whom the Son wishes to reveal him" (*Matthew* 11:25,27).

Prayer to the Father was the life breath of his earthly existence. He came to dwell in our midst but Jesus did not leave the house of the Father because he kept communion with him in prayer. On the other hand, however, this filial intimacy became a merciful and saving closeness for his brothers right up to the supreme sacrifice of the cross.

The prayer of Jesus continues still today (cf. *Hebrews* 7:25). In the Eucharistic liturgy, Christ the High Priest offers to the Father his redeeming sacrifice. He offers it in communion with his body which is the Church. Every prayer of ours is raised to the Father "through Christ our Lord". It is this prayer of Christ which sustains all our prayers, those spoken and those in the heart. When the Church prays, it is the Son who embraces the knees of the Father. The prayer of the sons ascends to the Father through the voice of the First Born. The arms raised up in invocation, praise, and supplication are millions but the voice is one alone, that of the Son.

This painting depicts Jesus at prayer in Gethsemane. He accepts the bitter cup of his passion in an act of supreme obedience to the Father for the salvation of mankind.

————————

EL GRECO, *Prayer of Jesus in the Garden*, Museum of Art, Toledo, Ohio.

578. What is the origin of the *Our Father*?

Jesus taught us this Christian prayer for which there is no substitute, the *Our Father*, on the day on which one of his disciples saw him praying and asked him, "Lord, teach us to pray" (*Luke* 11:1). The Church's liturgical tradition has always used the text of Saint Matthew (6:9-13).

2759-2760
2773

"THE SUMMARY OF THE WHOLE GOSPEL"

579. What is the place of the *Our Father* in the Scriptures?

The *Our Father* is the "summary of the whole Gospel" (Tertullian), "the perfect prayer" (Saint Thomas Aquinas). Found in the middle of the Sermon on the Mount (*Matthew* 5-7), it presents in the form of prayer the essential content of the Gospel.

2761-2764
2774

580. Why is it called the "Lord's Prayer"?

The *Our Father* is called the "Oratio Dominica", that is, the Lord's Prayer because it was taught to us by the Lord Jesus himself.

2765-2766
2775

581. What place does the *Our Father* have in the prayer of the Church?

The *Lord's Prayer* is the prayer of the Church *par excellence*. It is "handed on" in Baptism to signify the new birth of the children of God into the divine life. The full meaning of the *Our Father* is revealed in the Eucharist since its petitions are based on the mystery of salvation already accomplished, petitions that will be fully heard at the coming of the Lord. The *Our Father* is an integral part of the Liturgy of the Hours.

2767-2772
2776

"OUR FATHER WHO ART IN HEAVEN"

582. Why can we dare to draw near to God in full confidence?

Because Jesus, our Redeemer, brings us into the Father's presence and his Spirit makes us his children. We are thus able to pray the *Our Father* with simple and filial trust, with joyful assurance and humble boldness, with the certainty of being loved and heard.

2777-2778
2797

583. How is it possible to address God as "Father"?

We can invoke the "Father" because the Son of God made man has revealed him to us and because his Spirit makes him known to us. The invocation, "Father", lets us enter into his mystery with an ever new sense of wonder and awakens in us the desire to act as his children. When we pray the Lord's Prayer, we are therefore aware of our being sons of the Father in the Son.

2779-2785
2789
2798-2800

584. Why do we say "our" Father?

2786-2790
2801
"Our" expresses a totally new relationship with God. When we pray to the Father, we adore and glorify him with the Son and the Holy Spirit. In Christ we are "his" people and he is "our" God now and for eternity. In fact, we also say "our" Father because the Church of Christ is the communion of a multitude of brothers and sisters who have but "one heart and mind" (*Acts* 4:32).

585. With what spirit of communion and mission do we pray to God as "our" Father?

2791-2793
2801
Since praying to "our" Father is a common blessing for the baptised, we feel an urgent summons to join in Jesus' prayer for the unity of his disciples. To pray the "Our Father" is to pray with all people and for all people that they may know the one true God and be gathered into unity.

586. What does the phrase "Who art in heaven" mean?

2794-2796
2802
This biblical expression does not indicate a place but a way of being: God transcends everything. The expression refers to the majesty, the holiness of God, and also to his presence in the hearts of the just. Heaven, or the Father's house, constitutes our true homeland towards which we are moving in hope while we are still on earth. "Hidden with Christ in God" (*Colossians* 3:3), we live already in this homeland.

THE SEVEN PETITIONS

587. What is the structure of the Lord's Prayer?

2803-2806
2857
It contains seven petitions made to God the Father. The first three, more God-centered, draw us towards him for his glory; it is characteristic of love to think first of the beloved. These petitions suggest in particular what we ought to ask of him: the sanctification of his Name, the coming of his Kingdom, and the fulfillment of his will. The last four petitions present to the Father of mercies our wretchedness and our expectations. They ask him to feed us, to forgive us, to sustain us in temptations, and to free us from the Evil One.

588. What does "Hallowed be thy Name" mean?

2807-2812
2858
To hallow or make holy the Name of God is above all a prayer of praise that acknowledges God as holy. In fact, God revealed his holy Name to Moses and wanted *his* people to be consecrated for him as a holy nation in which he would dwell.

589. How is the Name of God made holy in us and in the world?

To make holy the Name of God, who calls us "to holiness" (1 *Thessalonians* 4:7) is to desire that our baptismal consecration animate our whole life. In addition, it is to ask - with our lives and our prayers - that the Name of God be known and blessed by every man.

2813-2815

590. What does the Church ask for when she prays "Thy Kingdom come"?

The Church prays for the final coming of the Kingdom of God through Christ's return in glory. The Church prays also that the Kingdom of God increase from now on through people's sanctification in the Spirit and through their commitment to the service of justice and peace in keeping with the Beatitudes. This petition is the cry of the Spirit and the Bride: "Come, Lord Jesus" (*Revelation* 22:20).

2816-2821
2859

591. Why pray "Thy will be done on earth as it is in heaven"?

The will of the Father is that "all men be saved" (1 *Timothy* 2:4). For this Jesus came: to perfectly fulfill the saving will of his Father. We pray God our Father to unite our will to that of his Son after the example of the Blessed Virgin Mary and the saints. We ask that this loving plan be fully realised on earth as it is already in heaven. It is through prayer that we can discern "what is the will of God" (*Romans* 12:2) and have the "steadfastness to do it" (*Hebrews* 10:36).

2822-2827
2860

592. What is the sense of the petition "Give us this day our daily bread"?

Asking God with the filial trust of children for the daily nourishment which is necessary for us all we recognise how good God is, beyond all goodness. We ask also for the grace to know how to act so that justice and solidarity may allow the abundance of some to remedy the needs of others.

2828-2834
2861

593. What is the specifically Christian sense of this petition?

Since "man does not live by bread alone but by every word that comes from the mouth of God" (*Matthew* 4:4), this petition equally applies to hunger for the *Word of God* and for the *Body of Christ* received in the Eucharist as well as hunger for the Holy Spirit. We ask this with complete confidence for *this day* - God's "today" - and this is given to us above all in the Eucharist which anticipates the banquet of the Kingdom to come.

2835-2837
2861

594. Why do we say "Forgive us our trespasses as we forgive those who trespass against us"?

2838-2839
2862

By asking God the Father to pardon us, we acknowledge before him that we are sinners. At the same time we proclaim his mercy because in his Son and through the sacraments "we have redemption, the forgiveness of sins" (*Colossians* 1:14). Still our petition will be answered only if we for our part have forgiven first.

595. How is forgiveness possible?

2840-2845
2862

Mercy can penetrate our hearts only if we ourselves learn how to forgive - even our enemies. Now even if it seems impossible for us to satisfy this requirement, the heart that offers itself to the Holy Spirit can, like Christ, love even to love's extreme; it can turn injury into compassion and transform hurt into intercession. Forgiveness participates in the divine mercy and is a high-point of Christian prayer.

596. What does "Lead us not into temptation" mean?

2846-2849
2863

We ask God our Father not to leave us alone and in the power of temptation. We ask the Holy Spirit to help us know how to discern, on the one hand, between a *trial* that makes us grow in goodness and a *temptation* that leads to sin and death and, on the other hand, between *being tempted* and *consenting* to temptation. This petition unites us to Jesus who overcame temptation by his prayer. It requests the grace of vigilance and of final perseverance.

597. Why do we conclude by asking "But deliver us from evil"?

2850-2854
2864

"Evil" indicates the person of Satan who opposes God and is "the deceiver of the whole world" (*Revelation* 12:9). Victory over the devil has already been won by Christ. We pray, however, that the human family be freed from Satan and his works. We also ask for the precious gift of peace and the grace of perseverance as we wait for the coming of Christ who will free us definitively from the Evil One.

598. What is the meaning of the final *Amen*?

2855-2856
2865

"At the end of the prayer, you say 'Amen' and thus you ratify by this word that means 'so be it' all that is contained in this prayer that God has taught us." (Saint Cyril of Jerusalem)

The angels are creatures of God. A part of them remained and remain faithful to him, in his presence, his service, and the service of the Church; and they are united with all the saved in the glory of heaven.

As in the vision of Jacob's ladder - "God's messengers were going up and down on it" (*Genesis* 28:12) - the angels are energetic and tireless messengers who connect heaven to earth. Between God and mankind there is not silence or a lack of communication but a continual conversation, a ceaseless personal exchange. Men, to whom this communication is addressed, have to sharpen their spiritual ear to hear and understand this angelic language which prompts good words, holy sentiments, acts of mercy, charitable behaviour, and edifying relationships.

It is this that we ask of our guardian angel in that well-known prayer of popular Catholic devotion:

"Angel of God, my guardian dear,
To whom God's love commits me here,
Ever this day be at my side
To light, to guard, to rule, and guide. Amen."

The image presented here portrays a group of apterous angels (that is, without wings) who pray by singing. They are dressed in sumptuous sacred vestments to indicate that they are discharging a solemn liturgical action. Indeed the angels, besides being messengers of God who are sent to declare his sovereign will to men, perform also the service of praising the Lord in the eternal liturgy of heaven (cf. *Revelation* 8:2).

JAN VAN EYCK, *Angelic Singers*, Polyptych in the Cathedral of Ghent.

APPENDIX

A) COMMON PRAYERS

B) FORMULAS OF CATHOLIC DOCTRINE

A) COMMON PRAYERS

The Sign of the Cross

In the name of the Father
and of the Son
and of the Holy Spirit. Amen.

Signum Crucis

In nómine Patris
et Fílii
et Spíritus Sancti. Amen.

Glory be to the Father

Glory be to the Father
and to the Son
and to the Holy Spirit.
As it was in the beginning,
is now, and ever shall be
world without end. Amen.

Gloria Patri

Glória Patri
et Fílio
et Spirítui Sancto.
Sicut erat in princípio,
et nunc et semper
et in sǽcula sæculórum. Amen.

The Hail Mary

Hail, Mary, full of grace,
the Lord is with thee.
Blessed art thou among women
and blessed is the fruit of thy
womb, Jesus.
Holy Mary, Mother of God,
pray for us sinners,
now and at the hour of our death.
Amen.

Ave, Maria

Ave, María, grátia plena,
Dóminus tecum.
Benedícta tu in muliéribus,
et benedíctus fructus ventris tui,
Iesus.
Sancta María, Mater Dei,
ora pro nobis peccatóribus,
nunc et in hora mortis nostræ.
Amen.

Angel of God

Angel of God,
my guardian dear,
to whom God's love commits me
here,
ever this day be at my side,
to light and guard,
to rule and guide.
Amen.

Angele Dei

Ángele Dei,
qui custos es mei,
me, tibi commíssum pietáte
supérna,
illúmina, custódi,
rege et gubérna.
Amen.

Eternal Rest

Eternal rest grant unto them,
O Lord,
and let perpetual light shine upon
them.
May they rest in peace. Amen.

Requiem Æternam

Réquiem ætérnam dona eis,
Dómine,
et lux perpétua lúceat eis.
Requiéscant in pace. Amen.

The Angelus

*V. The Angel of the Lord declared
unto Mary.*
R. And she conceived of the
Holy Spirit.
Hail Mary...
V. Behold the handmaid of the Lord.
R. Be it done unto me according
to thy word.
Hail Mary...
V. And the Word was made flesh.
R. And dwelt among us.
Hail Mary...
V. Pray for us, O holy Mother of God.
R. That we may be made worthy of
the promises of Christ.

Let us pray:
Pour forth, we beseech thee,
O Lord, thy grace into our hearts;
that we, to whom the Incarnation
of Christ, thy Son, was made known
by the message of an angel,
may by his Passion and Cross be
brought to the glory of his
Resurrection.
Through the same
Christ, our Lord. Amen.
Glory be...

Angelus Domini

*Ángelus Dómini
nuntiávit Maríæ.*
Et concépit
de Spíritu Sancto.
Ave, María...
Ecce ancílla Dómini.
Fiat mihi secúndum
verbum tuum.
Ave, María...
Et Verbum caro factum est.
Et habitávit in nobis.
Ave, María...
Ora pro nobis, sancta Dei génetrix.
Ut digni efficiámur
promissiónibus Christi.

Orémus.
Grátiam tuam, quǽsumus,
Dómine, méntibus nostris infúnde;
ut qui, Ángelo nuntiánte,
Christi Fílii tui incarnatiónem
cognóvimus,
per passiónem eius et crucem,
ad resurrectiónis glóriam
perducámur.
Per eúndem Christum
Dóminum nostrum. Amen.
Glória Patri...

The Regina Cæli

Queen of heaven, rejoice, alleluia!
For he whom you were worthy to bear, alleluia!
Has risen as he said, alleluia!
Pray for us to God, alleluia!
Rejoice and be glad, O Virgin Mary, alleluia!
For the Lord has risen indeed, alleluia!

Let us pray:

O God, who through the resurrection of your Son, our Lord Jesus Christ, did vouchsafe to give joy to the world; grant, we beseech you, that through his Mother, the Virgin Mary, we may obtain the joys of everlasting life. Through the same Christ our Lord. Amen.

Regina Cæli

Regína cæli lætáre, allelúia.
Quia quem meruísti portáre, allelúia.
Resurréxit, sicut dixit, allelúia.
Ora pro nobis Deum, allelúia.
Gaude et lætáre, Virgo María, allelúia.
Quia surréxit Dóminus vere, allelúia.

Orémus.

Deus, qui per resurrectiónem Fílii tui Dómini nostri Iesu Christi mundum lætificáre dignátus es, præsta, quǽsumus, ut per eius Genetrícem Vírginem Maríam perpétuæ capiámus gáudia vitæ.
Per Christum Dóminum nostrum. Amen.

Hail Holy Queen

Hail, Holy Queen, Mother of Mercy,
Hail our life,
our sweetness and our hope!
To thee do we cry, poor banished children of Eve.
To thee do we send up our sighs, mourning and weeping in this valley of tears!
Turn, then, most gracious Advocate, thine eyes of mercy towards us,
and after this, our exile,
show unto us the blessed fruit of thy womb, Jesus.
O clement, O loving,
O sweet Virgin Mary.

Salve, Regina

Salve, Regína,
Mater misericórdiæ,
vita, dulcédo et spes nostra, salve.
Ad te clamámus,
éxsules fílii Evæ.
Ad te suspirámus geméntes et flentes in hac lacrimárum valle.
Eia ergo, advocáta nostra,
illos tuos misericórdes óculos
ad nos convérte.
Et Iesum benedíctum fructum ventris tui,
nobis, post hoc exsílium, osténde.
O clemens, o pia,
o dulcis Virgo María!

The Magnificat

My soul glorifies the Lord,
My spirit rejoices in God
my Saviour.
He looks on his servant in her
lowliness;
Henceforth all generations will call
me blessed.
The Almighty works marvels for me.
Holy his name!
His mercy is from age to age,
on those who fear him.
He puts forth his arm in strength
And scatters the proud hearted.
He casts the mighty from their
thrones and raises the lowly.
He fills the starving with good things,
Sends the rich away empty.
He protects Israel, his servant,
remembering his mercy,
the mercy promised to our fathers,
to Abraham and his sons for ever.
Glory be to the Father and to the
Son and to the Holy Spirit.
As it was in the beginning, is now,
and ever shall be,
world without end. Amen.

Under Your Protection

We fly to thy protection,
O holy Mother of God.
Despise not our petitions in our
necessities,
but deliver us always from all dangers
O glorious and blessed Virgin.

Magnificat

Magníficat ánima mea Dóminum,
et exsultávit spíritus meus
in Deo salvatóre meo,
quia respéxit humilitátem
ancíllæ suæ.
Ecce enim ex hoc beátam
me dicent omnes generatiónes,
quia fecit mihi magna,
qui potens est,
et sanctum nomen eius,
et misericórdia eius in progénies
et progénies timéntibus eum.
Fecit poténtiam in bráchio suo,
dispérsit supérbos mente cordis sui;
depósuit poténtes de sede
et exaltávit húmiles.
Esuriéntes implévit bonis
et dívites dimísit inánes.
Suscépit Ísrael púerum suum,
recordátus misericórdiæ,
sicut locútus est ad patres nostros,
Ábraham et sémini eius in sǽcula.
Glória Patri et Fílio et Spirítui Sancto.
Sicut erat in princípio,
et nunc et semper,
et in sǽcula sæculórum. Amen.

Sub tuum præsidium

Sub tuum præsídium confúgimus,
sancta Dei Génetrix;
nostras deprecatiónes ne despícias
in necessitátibus;
sed a perículis cunctis
líbera nos semper,
Virgo gloriósa et benedícta.

The Benedictus

Blessed be the Lord,
the God of Israel!
He has visited his people and
redeemed them.
He has raised up for us a mighty
saviour
in the house of David his servant,
as he promised by the lips of
holy men,
those who were his prophets from
of old.
A saviour who would free us from
our foes,
from the hands of all who hate us.
So his love for our fathers is fulfilled
and his holy covenant remembered.
He swore to Abraham our father to
grant us,
that free from fear, and saved from
the hands of our foes,
we might serve him in holiness
and justice
all the days of our life in his
presence.
As for you, little child, you shall be
called a prophet of God,
the Most High.
You shall go ahead of the Lord,
to prepare his ways before him.
To make known to his people their
salvation,
through forgiveness of all their sins,
the loving-kindness of the heart of
our God,
who visits us like the dawn from
on high.

Benedictus

Benedíctus Dóminus,
Deus Ísrael,
quia visitávit
et fecit redemptiónem plebi suæ,
et eréxit cornu salútis nobis
in domo David púeri sui,
sicut locútus est per os sanctórum,
qui a sǽculo sunt,
prophetárum eius,
salútem ex inimícis nostris
et de manu ómnium,
qui odérunt nos;
ad faciéndam misericórdiam
cum pátribus nostris
et memorári testaménti sui sancti,
iusiurándum, quod iurávit
ad Ábraham patrem nostrum,
datúrum se nobis,
ut sine timóre,
de manu inimicórum liberáti,
serviámus illi
in sanctitáte et iustítia coram ipso
ómnibus diébus nostris.
Et tu, puer,
prophéta Altíssimi vocáberis:
præíbis enim ante fáciem Dómini
paráre vias eius,
ad dandam sciéntiam salútis
plebi eius
in remissiónem peccatórum eórum,
per víscera misericórdiæ
Dei nostri,
in quibus visitábit nos óriens ex alto,
illumináre his, qui in ténebris
et in umbra mortis sedent,
ad dirigéndos pedes nostros

He will give light to those
in darkness,
those who dwell in the shadow of
death,
and guide us into the way of peace.
Glory be to the Father and to the
Son and to the Holy Spirit.
As it was in the beginning, is now,
and ever shall be, world without
end. Amen.

in viam pacis.
Glória Patri et Fílio
et Spirítui Sancto.
Sicut erat in princípio,
et nunc
et semper,
et in sǽcula sæculórum.
Amen.

The Te Deum

We praise you, O God:
We acclaim you as Lord.
Everlasting Father,
All the world bows down before you.
All the angels sing your praise,
The hosts of heaven and all the
angelic powers,
All the cherubim and seraphim
Call out to you in unending song:
Holy, Holy, Holy,
Is the Lord God of angel hosts!
The heavens and the earth are filled
With your majesty and glory.
The glorious band of apostles,
The noble company of prophets,
The white-robed army who shed
their blood for Christ,
All sing your praise.
And to the ends of the earth
Your holy Church proclaims her
faith in you:
Father, whose majesty is boundless,
Your true and only Son, who is to
be adored,

Te Deum

Te Deum laudámus:
te Dóminum confitémur.
Te ætérnum Patrem,
omnis terra venerátur.
tibi omnes ángeli,
tibi cæli
et univérsæ potestátes:
tibi chérubim et séraphim
incessábili voce proclámant:
Sanctus, Sanctus, Sanctus,
Dóminus Deus Sábaoth.
Pleni sunt cæli et terra
maiestátis glóriæ tuæ.
Te gloriósus
apostolórum chorus,
te prophetárum
laudábilis númerus,
te mártyrum candidátus
laudat exércitus.
Te per orbem terrárum
sancta confitétur Ecclésia,
Patrem imménsæ maiestátis;
venerándum tuum verum
et únicum Fílium;

The Holy Spirit sent to be our Advocate.
You, Christ, are the king of glory,
Son of the eternal Father.
When you took our nature to save mankind
You did not shrink from birth in the Virgin's womb.
You overcame the power of death,
Opening the Father's kingdom to all who believe in you.
Enthroned at God's right hand in the glory of the Father,
You will come in judgment according to your promise.
You redeemed your people by your precious blood.
Come, we implore you, to our aid.
Grant us with the saints
a place in eternal glory.
Lord, save your people
And bless your inheritance.
Rule them and uphold them
For ever and ever.
Day by day we praise you:
We acclaim you now and to all eternity.
In your goodness, Lord, keep us free from sin.
Have mercy on us, Lord,
have mercy.
May your mercy always be with us, Lord,
For we have hoped in you.
In you, Lord, we put our trust:
We shall not be put to shame.

Sanctum quoque
Paráclitum Spíritum.
Tu rex glóriæ, Christe.
Tu Patris sempitérnus es Fílius.
Tu, ad liberándum susceptúrus hóminem,
non horruísti Vírginis úterum.
Tu, devícto mortis acúleo,
aperuísti credéntibus
regna cælórum.
Tu ad déxteram Dei sedes,
in glória Patris.
Iudex créderis esse ventúrus.
Te ergo quǽsumus,
tuis fámulis súbveni,
quos pretióso sánguine redemísti.
Ætérna fac cum sanctis tuis
in glória numerári.
Salvum fac pópulum tuum, Dómine,
et bénedic hereditáti tuæ.
Et rege eos, et extólle illos
usque in ætérnum.
Per síngulos dies benedícimus te;
et laudámus nomen tuum
in sǽculum, et in sǽculum sǽculi.
Dignáre, Dómine,
die isto sine peccáto nos custodíre.
Miserére nostri, Dómine, miserére nostri.
Fiat misericórdia tua,
Dómine, super nos,
quemádmodum sperávimus in te.
In te,
Dómine, sperávi:
non confúndar in ætérnum.

Come, Creator Spirit

Come, Holy Spirit, Creator come,
From your bright heavenly throne!
Come, take possession of our souls,
And make them all your own.

You who are called the Paraclete,
Best gift of God above,
The living spring, the living fire,
Sweet unction, and true love!

You who are sevenfold in your grace,
Finger of God's right hand,
His promise, teaching little ones
To speak and understand!

O guide our minds with your
blessed light,
With love our hearts inflame,
And with your strength which
never decays
Confirm our mortal frame.

Far from us drive our hellish foe
True peace unto us bring,
And through all perils guide us safe
Beneath your sacred wing.

Through you may we the Father
know,
Through you the eternal Son
And you the Spirit of them both
Thrice-blessed three in one.

All glory to the Father be,
And to the risen Son;
The same to you, O Paraclete,
While endless ages run. Amen.

Veni, Creator Spiritus

Veni, creátor Spíritus,
mentes tuórum vísita,
imple supérna grátia,
quæ tu creásti péctora.

Qui díceris Paráclitus,
altíssimi donum Dei,
fons vivus, ignis, cáritas,
et spiritális únctio.

Tu septifórmis múnere,
dígitus patérnæ déxteræ,
tu rite promíssum Patris,
sermóne ditans gúttura.

Accénde lumen sénsibus,
infúnde amórem córdibus,
infírma nostri córporis
virtúte firmans pérpeti.

Hostem repéllas lóngius
pacémque dones prótinus;
ductóre sic te prǽvio
vitémus omne nóxium.

Per Te sciámus da Patrem
noscámus atque Fílium,
teque utriúsque Spíritum
credámus omni témpore.

Deo Patri sit glória,
et Fílio, qui a mórtuis
surréxit, ac Paráclito,
in sæculórum sǽcula.
Amen.

Come, Holy Spirit

Come, Holy Spirit, come!
And from your celestial home
Shed a ray of light divine!

Come, Father of the poor!
Come, source of all our store!
Come, within our bosoms shine.

You, of comforters the best;
You, the soul's most welcome guest;
Sweet refreshment here below.

In our labour, rest most sweet;
Grateful coolness in the heat;
Solace in the midst of woe.

O most blessed Light divine,
Shine within these hearts of yours,
And our inmost being fill!

Where you are not, we have naught,
Nothing good in deed or thought,
Nothing free from taint of ill.

Heal our wounds, our strength renew;
On our dryness pour your dew;
Wash the stains of guilt away.

Bend the stubborn heart and will;
Melt the frozen, warm the chill;
Guide the steps that go astray.

On the faithful, who adore
And confess you, evermore
In your sevenfold gift descend.

Give them virtue's sure reward;
Give them your salvation, Lord;
Give them joys that never end. Amen.

Veni, Sancte Spiritus

Veni, Sancte Spíritus,
et emítte cǽlitus
lucis tuæ rádium.

Veni, pater páuperum,
veni, dator múnerum,
veni, lumen córdium.

Consolátor óptime,
dulcis hospes ánimæ,
dulce refrigérium.

In labóre réquies,
in æstu tempéries,
in fletu solácium.

O lux beatíssima,
reple cordis íntima
tuórum fidélium.

Sine tuo númine,
nihil est in hómine
nihil est innóxium.

Lava quod est sórdidum,
riga quod est áridum,
sana quod est sáucium.

Flecte quod est rígidum,
fove quod est frígidum,
rege quod est dévium.

Da tuis fidélibus,
in te confidéntibus,
sacrum septenárium.

Da virtútis méritum,
da salútis éxitum,
da perénne gáudium. Amen.

The Anima Christi

Soul of Christ, be my sanctification.
Body of Christ, be my salvation.
Blood of Christ, fill all my veins.
Water of Christ's side, wash out my stains.
Passion of Christ, my comfort be.
O good Jesu, listen to me.
In Thy wounds I fain would hide,
N'er to be parted from Thy side,
Guard me, should the foe assail me.
Call me when my life shall fail me.
Bid me come to Thee above,
With Thy saints to sing Thy love,
World without end. Amen.

Anima Christi

Ánima Christi, sanctífica me.
Corpus Christi, salva me.
Sanguis Christi, inébria me.
Aqua láteris Christi, lava me.
Pássio Christi, confórta me.
O bone Iesu, exáudi me.
Intra tua vúlnera abscónde me.
Ne permíttas me separári a te.
Ab hoste malígno defénde me.
In hora mortis meæ voca me.
Et iube me veníre ad te,
ut cum Sanctis tuis laudem te
in sǽcula sæculórum. Amen

The Memorare

Remember, O most gracious Virgin Mary, that never was it known that anyone who fled to thy protection, implored thy help, or sought thy intercession, was left unaided. Inspired by this confidence I fly unto thee, O Virgin of virgins, my Mother. To thee do I come, before thee I stand, sinful and sorrowful. O Mother of the Word Incarnate, despise not my petitions, but in thy mercy hear and answer me. Amen.

Memorare

Memoráre, o piíssima Virgo María, non esse audítum a sǽculo, quemquam ad tua curréntem præsídia, tua implorántem auxília, tua peténtem suffrágia, esse derelíctum. Ego tali animátus confidéntia, ad te, Virgo Vírginum, Mater, curro, ad te vénio, coram te gemens peccátor assísto.
Noli, Mater Verbi, verba mea despícere; sed áudi propítia et exáudi. Amen.

The Rosary

Rosarium

The Joyful Mysteries
(recited Monday and Saturday)

Mystéria gaudiósa
(in feria secunda et sabbato)

The Annunciation.
The Visitation.
The Nativity.
The Presentation.
The Finding in the Temple.

Annuntiátio.
Visitátio.
Natívitas.
Præsentátio.
Invéntio in Templo.

The Mysteries of Light
(recited Thursday)

Mystéria luminósa
(in feria quinta)

The Baptism of Jesus.
The Wedding Feast of Cana.
The Proclamation of the Kingdom
with the call to Conversion.
The Transfiguration.
The Institution of the Eucharist.

Baptísma apud Iordánem.
Autorevelátio apud Cananénse
matrimónium.
Regni Dei proclamátio coniúncta
cum invitaménto ad conversiónem.
Transfigurátio.
Eucharístiæ Institútio.

The Sorrowful Mysteries
(recited Tuesday and Friday)

Mystéria dolorósa
(in feria tertia et feria sexta)

The Agony in the Garden.
The Scourging at the Pillar.
The Crowning with Thorns.
The Carrying of the Cross.
The Crucifixion and Death.

Agonía in Hortu.
Flagellátio.
Coronátio Spinis.
Baiulátio Crucis.
Crucifíxio et Mors.

The Glorious Mysteries
(recited Wednesday and Sunday)

Mystéria gloriósa
(in feria quarta et Dominica)

The Resurrection.
The Ascension.
The Descent of the Holy Spirit.
The Assumption.
The Coronation of Mary Queen of
Heaven and Earth.

Resurréctio.
Ascénsio.
Descénsus Spíritus Sancti.
Assúmptio.
Coronátio in Cælo.

Prayer concluding the Rosary

Oratio ad finem Rosarii dicenda

Hail, Holy Queen, etc. as above

V. *Pray for us, O holy Mother of God.*

R. That we may be made worthy of the promises of Christ.

Let us pray:

O God, whose only-begotten Son, by his life, death and resurrection, has purchased for us the rewards of eternal life, grant, we beseech thee, that meditating on these mysteries of the most holy Rosary of the Blessed Virgin Mary, we may imitate what they contain and obtain what they promise, through the same Christ our Lord. Amen.

Ora pro nobis, sancta Dei génetrix.

Ut digni efficiámur promissiónibus Christi.

Orémus.

Deus, cuius Unigénitus per vitam, mortem et resurrectiónem suam nobis salútis ætérnæ præmia comparávit, concéde, quæsumus: ut hæc mystéria sacratíssimo beátæ Maríæ Vírginis Rosário recoléntes, et imitémur quod cóntinent, et quod promíttunt assequámur.

Per Christum Dóminum nostrum. Amen.

Coptic Incense Prayer

O King of peace, give us your peace and pardon our sins. Dismiss the enemies of the Church and protect her so that she may never fail. Emmanuel our God is in our midst in the glory of the Father and of the Holy Spirit. May he bless us and purify our hearts and cure the sicknesses of our soul and body. We adore you, O Christ, with your good Father and the Holy Spirit because you have come and you have saved us.

Syro-Maronite Farewell to the Altar

Remain in peace, O Altar of God. May the offering that I have taken from you be for the remission of my debts and the pardon of my sins and may it obtain for me that I may stand before the tribunal of Christ without condemnation and without confusion. I do not know if I will have the opportunity to return and offer another sacrifice upon you. Protect me, O Lord, and preserve your holy Church as the way to truth and salvation. Amen.

Byzantine Prayer for the Deceased

God of the spirits and of all flesh, who have trampled death and annihilated the devil and given life to your world, may you yourself, O Lord, grant to the soul of your deceased servant N. rest in a place of light, a verdant place, a place of freshness, from where suffering, pain and cries are far removed. May You, O good and compassionate God forgive every fault committed by him in word, work or thought because there is no man who lives and does not sin. You alone are without sin and your justice is justice throughout the ages and your word is truth. Since you, O Christ our God, are the resurrection, the life and the repose of your deceased servant N., we give you glory together with your un-begotten Father and your most holy, good and life-creating Spirit, now and always and forever and ever. Amen

Act of Faith

O my God, I firmly believe that you are one God in three divine Persons, Father, Son, and Holy Spirit. I believe that your divine Son became man and died for our sins and that he will come to judge the living and the dead. I believe these and all the truths which the Holy Catholic Church teaches because you have revealed them who are eternal truth and wisdom, who can neither deceive nor be deceived. In this faith I intend to live and die. Amen.

Actus fidei

Dómine Deus, firma fide credo et confíteor ómnia et síngula quæ sancta Ecclésia Cathólica propónit, quia tu, Deus, ea ómnia revelásti, qui es ætérna véritas et sapiéntia quæ nec fállere nec falli potest. In hac fide vívere et mori státuo. Amen.

Act of Hope

O Lord God, I hope by your grace for the pardon of all my sins and after life here to gain eternal happiness because you have promised it who are infinitely powerful, faithful, kind, and merciful. In this hope I intend to live and die. Amen.

Actus spei

Dómine Deus, spero per grátiam tuam remissiónem ómnium peccatórum, et post hanc vitam ætérnam felicitátem me esse consecutúrum: quia tu promisísti, qui es infiníte potens, fidélis, benígnus, et miséricors. In hac spe vívere et mori státuo. Amen.

Act of Love

O Lord God, I love you above all things and I love my neighbour for your sake because you are the highest, infinite and perfect good, worthy of all my love. In this love I intend to live and die. Amen.

Actus caritatis

Dómine Deus, amo te super ómnia et próximum meum propter te, quia tu es summum, infinítum, et perfectíssimum bonum, omni dilectióne dignum. In hac caritáte vívere et mori státuo. Amen.

Act of Contrition

O my God, I am heartily sorry for having offended Thee, and I detest all my sins because of thy just punishments, but most of all because they offend Thee, my God, who art all good and deserving of all my love. I firmly resolve with the help of Thy grace to sin no more and to avoid the near occasion of sin. Amen.

Actus contritionis

Deus meus, ex toto corde pænitet me ómnium meórum peccatórum, éaque detéstor, quia peccándo, non solum pœnas a te iuste statútas proméritus sum, sed præsértim quia offéndi te, summum bonum, ac dignum qui super ómnia diligáris. Ídeo fírmiter propóno, adiuvánte grátia tua, de cétero me non peccatúrum peccandíque occasiónes próximas fugitúrum. Amen.

B) FORMULAS OF CATHOLIC DOCTRINE

The two commandments of love

1. You shall love the Lord your God with all your heart, with all your soul, and with all your mind.
2. You shall love your neighbour as yourself.

The Golden Rule (*Mt* 7:12)

Do to others as you would have them do to you.

The Beatitudes (*Mt* 5:3-12)

Blessed are the poor in spirit,
for theirs is the kingdom of heaven.
Blessed are they who mourn,
for they will be comforted.
Blessed are the meek, for they will inherit the earth.
Blessed are they who hunger and thirst for righteousness,
for they will be satisfied.
Blessed are the merciful,
for they will be shown mercy.
Blessed are the pure of heart,
for they will see God.
Blessed are the peacemakers, for they will be called children of God.
Blessed are those who are persecuted for righteousness' sake, for theirs is the kingdom of heaven.
Blessed are you when people revile you and persecute you and utter all kinds of evil against you falsely on my account. Rejoice and be glad, for your reward will be great in heaven.

The three theological virtues

1. Faith
2. Hope
3. Charity

The four cardinal virtues

1. Prudence
2. Justice
3. Fortitude
4. Temperance

The seven gifts of the Holy Spirit

1. Wisdom
2. Understanding
3. Counsel
4. Fortitude
5. Knowledge
6. Piety
7. Fear of the Lord

The twelve fruits of the Holy Spirit

1. Charity
2. Joy
3. Peace
4. Patience
5. Kindness
6. Goodness
7. Generosity
8. Gentleness
9. Faithfulness
10. Modesty
11. Self-control
12. Chastity

The five precepts of the Church

1. You shall attend Mass on Sundays and on holy days of obligation and remain free from work or activity that could impede the sanctification of such days.
2. You shall confess your sins at least once a year.
3. You shall receive the sacrament of the Eucharist at least during the Easter season.
4. You shall observe the days of fasting and abstinence established by the Church.
5. You shall help to provide for the needs of the Church.

The seven corporal works of mercy

1. Feed the hungry.
2. Give drink to the thirsty.
3. Clothe the naked.
4. Shelter the homeless.
5. Visit the sick.
6. Visit the imprisoned.
7. Bury the dead.

The seven spiritual works of mercy

1. Counsel the doubtful.
2. Instruct the ignorant.
3. Admonish sinners.
4. Comfort the afflicted.
5. Forgive offences.
6. Bear wrongs patiently.
7. Pray for the living and the dead.

The seven capital sins

1. Pride
2. Covetousness
3. Lust
4. Anger
5. Gluttony
6. Envy
7. Sloth

The four last things

1. Death
2. Judgment
3. Hell
4. Heaven

ANALYTICAL INDEX

Numbers refer to the questions and answers

R

Picture Credits

PAGES 16 AND 17: *Adoration of the Magi* (altarpiece) (detail of 29414) by Fabriano, Gentile da (c.1370-1427), Galleria degli Uffizi, Florence, Italy / The Bridgeman Art Library

PAGE 21: Ms 1 f.4v *The Creation of the World*, from the Souvigny Bible (vellum) by French School, (12th century), Bibliotheque Municipale, Moulins, France / Lauros / Giraudon / The Bridgeman Art Library

PAGE 31: *Mosaic in the apsidal vault*, Rome, Church of San Clemente. © 1990. Photo Scala, Florence

PAGE 73: *The Last Supper* or, *The Communion of the Apostles*, 1474 (oil on panel) by Joos van Gent (Joos van Wassenhove) (fl.1460-75), Galleria Nazionale delle Marche, Urbino, Italy / Alinari / The Bridgeman Art Library

PAGES 86 AND 87: *The Altarpiece of the Seven Sacraments*, c.1445-50 (oil on panel) by Weyden, Rogier van der (1399-1464), Koninklijk Museum voor Schone Kunsten, Antwerp, Belgium / Giraudon / The Bridgeman Art Library

PAGE 109: Courtesy of the Most Rev Abbot, Mechitaristen, Vienna

PAGE 113: *The Immaculate Conception Contemplated by St John the Evangelist* (oil on panel) by Greco, El (Domenico Theotocopuli) (1541-1614), Museo de Santa Cruz, Toledo, Spain / The Bridgeman Art Library

PAGE 129: *The Sermon on the Mount*, 1442 (fresco) by Angelico, Fra (Guido di Pietro) (c.1387-1455), Museo di San Marco dell'Angelico, Florence, Italy / The Bridgeman Art Library

PAGE 169: *The Agony in the Garden*, about 1590-95 (oil on canvas), El Greco (1541-1614), Toledo Museum of Art

PAGE 175: *Singing Angels*, from the left wing of the Ghent Altarpiece, 1432 (oil on panel) by Eyck, Hubert (c.1370-1426) & Jan van (1390-1441), St Bavo Cathedral, Ghent, Belgium / The Bridgeman Art Library